TEACH YOUR

CHILD TO READ

IN JUST TEN

MINUTES A DAY

Sidney Ledson

TEACH YOUR CHILD TO READ IN JUST TEN MINUTES A DAY

Mentiscopic Publishing Co. Limited

Printed in Victoria, Canada.

First published in 1999 by Stoddart Publishing Co. Limited.
Revised edition published in 2003 by Mentiscopic Publishing Co. Limited
46 Minnacote Avenue, Toronto, Canada M1E 4B3.

Cover design and illustrations throughout the book: Essel
Text design: Tannice Goddard

Note for Librarians: a cataloguing record for this book that includes Dewey Classification and US Library of Congress numbers is available from the National Library of Canada. The complete cataloguing record can be obtained from the National Library's online database at: www.nlc-bnc.ca/amicus/index-e.html
ISBN 1-4120-1554-5

TRAFFORD

This book was published *on-demand* in cooperation with Trafford Publishing. On-demand publishing is a unique process and service of making a book available for retail sale to the public taking advantage of on-demand manufacturing and Internet marketing. **On-demand publishing** includes promotions, retail sales, manufacturing, order fulfilment, accounting and collecting royalties on behalf of the author.

Suite 6E, 2333 Government St., Victoria, B.C. V8T 4P4, CANADA
Phone   250-383-6864   Toll-free   1-888-232-4444 (Canada & US)
Fax   250-383-6804   E-mail   sales@trafford.com
Web site   www.trafford.com TRAFFORD PUBLISHING IS A DIVISION OF TRAFFORD HOLDINGS LTD.
Trafford Catalogue #03-1931   www.trafford.com/robots/03-1931.html

10   9   8   7   6   5   4   3   2   1

To the memory of my sister, Elsie Hill

Books by the same author

Educational
Raising Brighter Children

Humor
Scratch 'n Win

Talk About a Bad Hair Day
(pen name, Sister Trillium)

Simon Says (Sister Trillium)

(www.ledsonbooks.com)

Contents

PART TWO: TEACHING THE FIRST 100 WORDS

Acknowledgments

My thanks to editors Elizabeth d'Anjou, Gillian Watts, and Natalia Denesiuk for making this book more interesting and easier to read. Thanks also to Professor Patrick Groff for sage counsel.

Introduction

In an age when most things are sensationally new, or high-tech, and sometimes both, one might question the presentation of a reading method that is remarkably low-tech and yawningly old — a method dating back to the era of butter-churns and foot-treadle sewing machines. No matter. The method has a singular saving grace. It works one-hundred percent of the time. I speak of the phonic reading method.

Phonic systems of the past were designed for teaching school-age children. However, by reducing this time-tested method to a simpler form, I have created a reading system that allows you, with no formal training and little preparation, to teach almost anyone to read — including children previously thought too young to begin reading. Bearing in mind that the phonic method was highly successful long before I began tinkering with it thirty years ago, my revisions might be seen as no more than the fitting of new strings on a Stradivarius.

My fascination with ways to accelerate learning began in 1961, long before I entered the field of education. Eventually, in 1972, I decided to teach my own two- and three-year-old children what schoolteachers had taught me: that letters stand for sounds. Our lessons took the form of games. So, from my children's standpoint, learning to read was incidental to their engaging in various playful activities.

Because I had never taught before, the children's instruction was an explorative venture, one that — to my surprise — led to their passing, in just two months, a reading test for grade 1 children. This test, devised by a noted researcher, is shown on page 221.

The success of our reading venture prompted me to write the book *Teach Your Child to Read in 60 Days*. But the title was wrong. It should have been *Teach Your Child to Read in 46 Days*. Why? During our home program I began to doubt the correctness of my unprofessional teaching methods, and changed to one advised by a well-known advocate of early reading. His was a flashcard, "look-say," or "whole word" method (a method now entrenched in schools as part of the widely used "whole language" program). But, after two weeks of trying to memorize words (as the whole word method requires), my children were often guessing. I wanted reading, not guessing, so we changed back to my improvised phonic program. The two weeks we wasted in pursuing the faulty word-memorization method were wrongly counted among the sixty days in the title of the book.

After the book was published in 1975, thousands of parents successfully taught their children to read as I had taught mine. Many wrote to me. Their letters confirmed that the title was incorrect: "Thanks to your method, my child was reading in fifty days." Others said forty days, some, thirty days or twenty days, and one man, Michael J. Hardester of St. Louis, taught his youngster to read in *eleven* days (possibly a world record).

Was force used? You bet. Mr. Hardester's daughter — then in kindergarten — was so delighted with the reading game, she compelled her father to play it more often and longer than he intended.

The program presented here is much improved over the one Michael Hardester and other parents used years ago, which makes me believe that soon, when you are reading bedtime stories to your child, he or she will give you an occasional rest and read the story to you. One book in particular that your child will soon read is presented in part 4: "A Busy Day for Helpful Andrew." You might like to look at it now to see the level of reading your pupil or pupils will soon achieve.

A simplified method is monumentally important for quick and easy teaching, but entertainment is important too. So, engaging methods of presentation have been liberally shuffled into our instructional deck to guarantee you a winning hand at teaching, and your child a winning hand at learning.

Get ready for an adventure in reading instruction. If you haven't taught a child to read before, good. You will have no misconceptions, no favored beliefs, no practised errors to unlearn. The simple, motivationally enriched procedures described in this book have already given thousands of children the pleasures of early reading ability, plus the other rare advantages that invariably accompany early reading — advantages you can now easily give to your child.

THE PHONIC
READING METHOD

Introduction to Part One

What is the phonic reading method and why is it regarded so highly for teaching reading? You will more easily understand the value of this method if we consider the important role the phonic system plays in *your* ability to read.

Chances are, you learned to read so long ago that the initial puzzlements and eventual discoveries that permitted you to read are long forgotten. Converting print into thought has become second nature to you, so you are probably unaware of the skills and knowledge you are using right now to lift meaning from these words.

First, you know you must start at the left side of each word and work across to the right side. Nothing profound here. So simple, in fact, that it's hardly worth mentioning — except that some reading programs don't bother to tell children this. So, with the important left-to-right procedure untaught, picked up only incidentally, and insecurely fixed in pupils' minds, they sometimes read backwards — and are then labelled learning disadvantaged, dyslexic, or strephosymbolic.

What else do you know about reading? You might be surprised to know you have remarkable skill in attaching sounds to letters and letter combinations. I can help you prove this to yourself. Read the word below out loud. Go ahead.

ELEPHANT

You knew what sound to give the *E*. And the *L* presented no problem. Nor did the second *E*. Then you knew from past experience that the appropriate sound to give the combination of letters *PH* is the same as the sound beginning the word "fall." And the *A*, the *N*, and the *T* all represent sounds you know too. Simple.

This is what you know that non-readers don't know. And when we teach non-readers these two basic matters — the connection that exists between letters and sounds, and the need to read from left to right — then, whether they are age two, three, seven, or seventy, they will be able to read. Reading is as simple as that.

The reading method in this book is a phonic one. *Phonic* means "having to do with sound." We run into the word — or most of it — in the words *phonograph* (sound-writing), *telephone* (distant sound), *symphony* (agreement of sound), and *euphony* (pleasant sound). The series of letters you are reading at this moment convey to you the same sounds you would hear if I were speaking to you.

A line of letters set down on paper — as is done here — is really a sound-strip: a strip of sound symbols that you are translating into sound in your head without even realizing it. Read the limerick below for further proof.

> One bliss for which
> There is no match
> Is when you itch
> To up and scratch.*

You enjoyed the rhymes in the limerick even though you didn't read the words out loud. You transposed printed letters into sounds

---

* Ogden Nash

without conscious effort. Letters, and the sounds represented by letters, are what reading is all about. Nothing more. Nothing less. Regardless of what system is used to teach someone to read, the learner will never get the hang of reading until he or she is taught or discovers that letters on a page are stand-ins for the sounds of speech.

You may be both surprised and puzzled to learn that this simple and logical approach to reading isn't used in most schools. You might then wonder just how children are taught to read in most classrooms. They are taught by a whole word method, now popularly called the whole language method. Children learn to memorize an entire word — as a lump — instead of learning the sounds of the letters in the word. The basic assumption in this teaching method is that children learn to read by reading, in the same way they learn to skate by skating. And so, children begin memorizing the words in short sentences that ultimately make up a story. Because whole language programs give minimal or incidental attention to the letters in each word, children are naturally handicapped when they try to puzzle out words they haven't yet memorized. In fact, children are often taught to sound the first letter in a word, and then guess what the word is.

Whole language reading methods start out with a deceptive promise of quick reading advancement — deceptive because, though children are soon reading, their reading advancement is limited by the number of words they can memorize in a school year, and the stories they are given to read are written in a tightly controlled, low-count vocabulary, with words repeated as often as possible to aid memorization and recognition. Accordingly, reading progress tends to be slow and the reading material dull: "Look, look, I see a dog."

Some grade 2 and 3 public school children who begin attending the remedial reading clinic at the Sidney Ledson Institute can't read the word *elephant*. No one has told them that a *p* and an *h* can represent the speech-sound *f*. Fortunately, some children are bright enough to figure out the missing details on their own. But others, confused, conclude that reading is more work than pleasure, and settle for no-hassle TV — an insidious detour that leads to functional illiteracy and apparent dyslexia.

What is functional illiteracy? This is the sad state of one who, having memorized a number of words, employs sufficient coping tricks to give the appearance of being able to read, yet who can't puzzle out the meaning of printed matter encountered in daily life — a menu, a medicine label, an employment ad, or a public notice.

And dyslexia? Misuse of this term represents possibly the unkindest prank played by educators on unsuspecting parents and their children (though *learning disadvantaged* runs a close second). We are led to believe by some experts that the incidence of dyslexia has risen to near plague proportions. By some estimates, ten percent of children suffer from dyslexia.

Years ago I visited a doctor because I had a sore tongue. Whether this was the result of having eaten highly spiced food, abrasive food, a too hot soup, or what, I forget. But I recall being greatly impressed when the doctor merely glanced in my mouth and quick as a wink diagnosed the ailment as stomatitis. I remained impressed until I got home and looked up the meaning of *stomatitis*. It means "sore tongue." The doctor had merely taken the information I had given him and handed it back to me, gift-packaged with a fancy title.

The word *dyslexia* plays a similarly dysfunctional role in school communication. If a schoolchild is having difficulty reading, and an expert diagnoses dyslexia, the expert is merely gift-packaging. He is stating in a fancy way what is already known and obvious. Dyslexia means "a disturbance in the ability to read," something anyone would suffer by trying to read a newspaper on a roller coaster.

But gradually, and regrettably, in educational bafflegab the term *dyslexia* has taken on the meaning of "affliction," or "ailment." This tends to load the burden of a reading difficulty onto the child's own back, providing great relief for educators, who can then say, "We tried our best, but the child has dyslexia."

Of course, many children eventually learn to read even when faulty programs are used. A knowledgeable teacher who understands the key skills required for reading can compensate for the failings of any program. And so the caliber of the teacher is more important than the caliber of the reading program he or she is given to use. As the legendary teaching wizard of Westside Preparatory School in Chicago, Marva Collins, says, "All you really need for teaching is a blackboard, books, and a pair of legs that will last through the day" — and, we might add, the knowledge of letter sounds that Marva Collins and all other highly successful teachers have.*

When, in the best of all situations, a skilful teacher has a first-rate reading program to work with, truly remarkable reading achievement is possible, as will be seen in chapter 1.

Instruction throughout this book takes the form of "packages." You may wish to read only those parts of the book that deal with your particular teaching goal. If so, read chapters 1 and 2, then chapter 3 (which deals with teaching a preschooler), and finally, one of the following chapters:

- for babysitters and caregivers, chapter 4;
- for daycare and nursery school teachers, chapter 5;
- for kindergarten and grade 1 teachers, chapter 6;
- for parents wishing to teach a school-age child or correct a schoolchild's faulty reading, chapter 7.

But please note: every chapter contains ideas and suggestions that have relevance to your special teaching task and will advance your skills. You are urged to read the whole book.

Now you might like to meet some of our very young readers, as described in chapter 1.

---

* For years, Marva Collins (whose selfless work with inner-city children inspired the film *The Marva Collins Story*) championed the cause of the Reading Reform Foundation, a group dedicated to replacing whole word and whole language reading systems in public schools with the no-fail phonic reading method.

1

Getting Started

At the Sidney Ledson Institute for Intellectual Advancement, in Toronto, Mitchell Au, age two, peers into a thin book. This is the Ledson *First Reader*, containing a 114-word vocabulary in 96 sentences. Mitchell reads aloud in a clear, confident voice:

SIT ON THE RUG

WHERE IS THE WAGON?

DON'T JIGGLE THE JELLY

He smiles at this last sentence. Mitchell delights in reading — not just in reading our *First Reader*, which he has almost finished after seven months of half-day attendance, but any word he encounters, as in flyers delivered to his home, or the makes and models of cars he sees on the road. Mitchell is tuned in and turned on to reading, and thoroughly enjoys the communications rewards of his newly acquired skill.

In the chair beside him is Stephen Zhao, also age two. Like Mitchell, Stephen speaks Chinese at home. He understood little English when he joined us ten months ago. Now he, too, confidently reads sentences that would give many six-year-olds in public school trouble:

HERE ARE TEN BLOCKS

LOOK AT THAT FOX

WE HAVE A TELEVISION SET

A group of children seated on the floor in an adjoining room watch as the teacher holds up a succession of plaques bearing words in large letters. "Who can sound this out for me?" she asks. Every hand shoots up. The selected child sounds the individual letters, then, brimming with confidence, reads the word **BAG**. She hasn't guessed the word, she has *read* it, and she knows she's right. When the teacher gets up for a moment to greet a visitor, self-appointed assistant teacher Ika Washington — age three — seizes her chance. "I'll help," she declares, and holds up a word tablet for the group. "Who can read this word for me?" Her classmates laugh, but they all raise their hands. They want to keep the game going.

Moving along to the grade 1 classroom, we find youngsters engaging in chess and other thought-provoking activities. Six-year-old Laurence Batmazian, who has attended our school for two-and-a-half years, reads at grade 6.6 level (equivalent to a child who has been in grade 6 for 6 months). Laurence has finished H. G. Wells's *The Invisible Man* and is now deep in another classic, R. L. Stevenson's *Treasure Island*. This youngster can choose any book and easily read a hundred pages without stopping. His intelligence? Laurence's parents speak of his love of mind-challenging activities: crossword puzzles, word searches, mazes, and general problem-solving. Additionally, they report, "He always impresses people with his ability to discuss subjects in a mature manner, and remembers conversations and discussions with enviable recollection of what was said and done by who and where." (Memory exercises are part of the program at the Institute.)

Laurence demonstrates genius-level intelligence. This doesn't surprise us. After all, the primary goal at the Instutute is to raise children's intelligence, not just to dispense early instruction. The academic excellence our preschoolers exhibit is incidental to our main goal — increasing their intelligence — and is, therefore, virtually a spinoff. Nevertheless, of the various ways we stimulate intellectual activity and neural growth, reading instruction plays an exceedingly important role. The link between early reading ability and superior intelligence has been confirmed repeatedly throughout history. The early reading skill our pupils demonstrate is their ticket to intellectual advancement.

Consider also Safina Allidina, who has been with us since she was two. Now in our grade 1 classroom, Safina, age four, engages in her latest triumph — multiplication. Her reading ability is such that when her family dines out, she stuns waitresses by reading the menu and requesting her preferred dishes unaided. Recently, at a community gathering, Safina calmly read a half-page address to a group of five hundred people with neither hesitation nor concern (though her mother was nervous).

Some might think we are merely advancing the intelligence of already precocious children. Not so. We have no admissions test, so the children we work with are probably not much different from those in your home, or group, or class. Not much different, that is, when they enter our program. Then changes occur.

Mitchell, Stephen, Laurence, Safina, and others demonstrate the intellectual reach ordinary children can achieve when they reccive a rich early education, which, at the Institute, is the product of special instruction plus parent support and contribution.

Every child at the Sidney Ledson Institute learns to read. Every one — even the occasional child with Down syndrome. Each child reads with precision and enthusiasm. There are no reading failures, no reluctant readers. Guessing while reading is unknown. (And so is dyslexia, discussed further in Appendix I, "The Myth of Dyslexia.")

How much reading instruction do our children get? About ten minutes a day.

But that's not completely true. Few two- and three-year-olds attend the Institute all day. They attend either in the mornings or the afternoons. Many of these youngsters therefore get only five minutes of instruction each day. Then again, some attend school only three times a week. These children receive only fifteen minutes of instruction each week.

Yet they all read.

There's no magic here. The systematized, simplified reading program my teachers use — the same one presented in this book — resulted from a collaboration between myself and top authorities on the methods best suited for teaching very young children to read. These authorities were the thousand or so preschoolers who, having attended the Institute during a twenty-three-year period, indicated — by their speedy progress or by their puzzlement — what should be included in the program, or altered, or omitted. The result is a reading program extensively tested and approved by two- and three-year-olds.

With this program, Good Reader, you can give your own child quick literacy plus all the advantages that accompany learning to read, and you may do so without leaving your home or paying a tuition fee.

I repeat: there is no magic. A small amount of patience, an engaging manner of presentation, and the foolproof phonic system described in this book will work as well for you as it does for my teachers and their young charges. Give just ten minutes a day to the method and you will teach your preschooler to read while you are also stimulating his or her intellectual growth.

The program will also permit parents of older children to accelerate their children's reading progress, or to remedy their faulty reading. And the special instructions given for kindergarten and grade 1 teachers will permit them to graduate an entire class of wholly literate children at the end of just one school year — each pupil able to read and understand all the words in his or her speech vocabulary. Instruction is also included for those who work with daycare and nursery school children.

And lastly, detailed and specific instructions will enable teenage babysitters and homemakers who provide daycare in their homes to teach reading as an attractive feature of their child-minding service, or as an option to be provided at additional cost.

But first, perhaps we should address some oft voiced questions.

OF WHAT VALUE IS READING ABILITY TO A PRESCHOOLER?

A good question — and one with more answers than might be expected.

First, children who can read aren't dependent upon the presence and mood of an adult to enjoy their favorite stories. They can read the books of their choice unaided.

Second, children who can read have a welcome alternative to watching TV. A tragic consequence of delaying literacy to age six or seven is that, by that time, TV has usually assumed a dominant role in a child's lifestyle and is then a source of entertainment that can be difficult to dislodge or reduce in favor of reading.

Third, the world becomes a safer place for children who can read and understand warnings such as *POISON, DANGER, STOP,* and *BEWARE OF DOG.*

Fourth, when children are taught by the phonic or letter code method (the method we will be using), they discover sounds that are often omitted in popular speech — for example, the *G* in the *-ing* endings of words. As a consequence of their discoveries, children begin to incorporate these truant sounds into their speech, and their pronunciation improves.

Fifth, children yearn to know what is happening around them. Surrounded as we are by print, the ability to read signs, labels, flyers, and posters gives youngsters a satisfying fact-finding ability. Literacy is the equivalent of a sixth sense.

The sixth, and possibly most important, reason is the influence early literacy is seen to have on intelligence and academic success. The early reader seems to be stamped with intellectual brilliance as surely and routinely as if it had been punched up on a heavenly computer by divine command. As long ago as 1962, a study of four hundred eminent people found early reading ability to be a common characteristic of these high achievers. Many of the people studied were reading by age four.*

There's nothing new here. Throughout history, the upper levels of academic achievement have invariably been established by those who were taught to read before they entered school. Indeed, early readers often achieved eminence. Voltaire, David Lloyd George, and Thomas Babington Macaulay had all been taught to read by age three. Jonathan Swift, Samuel Johnson, and John Stuart Mill were reading by age two. Other members of this elite preschool alumni association include William James Sidis, Lord Kelvin, and Norbert Wiener, who entered college or university at the ages, respectively, of eleven, ten, and eleven. Their parents found nothing unusual about their children's high intelligence. In fact, parents have sometimes stated they could secure the same result with any child, given the opportunity. One parent, Aaron Stern, whose daughter Edith (IQ 200) is the subject of his book *The Making of a Genius* (Renaissance Publications, 1971), stated he could foster the same meteoric IQ in children of the Tasaday tribe, a Stone Age people living in the Philippines. (Unfortunately, he was unable to obtain custody of two Tasaday children to prove his assertion.)

But let's look now at a situation in which there can be no argument about what is effecting what: the education of children with brain damage. Specialists at the Institutes for the Achievement of Human Potential, in Philadelphia, pioneered procedures for improving the condition of brain-damaged children. At first, surgery was used to stop damaged areas of the brain from interfering with healthy areas. In its most invasive form, the surgery entailed hemispherectomy — the removal of an entire half of the child's brain. Then the team discovered that when half-brained children were engaged in intellectually stimu-

---

* V. Goertzel and M. G. Goertzel, *Cradles of Eminence* (Little, Brown & Co., 1962). A seminal work on this topic, *Children Who Read Early*, by Dolores Durkin (Teachers College Press, 1966), disclosed in two studies — one in Oakland, one in New York — that children who could read on entering school remained ahead of all others through to grade 6, where the study ended.

lating activities, their intelligence rose to the level of normal children's.

That was their first surprise.

Next, the experts discovered that children with *diseased* brains — containing millions of worthless cells — could similarly be normalized by intellectual stimulation alone, without surgery. Here was another surprise.

Then the team discovered that reading instruction provided a particularly powerful form of intellectual stimulation, one that worked almost like a deep-brain massage; and one that, while conferring the valuable gift of literacy, provided a bonus of inestimably greater value than literacy itself: heightened intelligence.

No surprise there. At least there shouldn't have been. Early reading instruction has figured so prominently in all documented cases of "manufactured" geniuses (children whose parents engaged them in a planned program of mind expansion) that the information is yawningly familiar to students of epistemology. Some of those parents predicted their child's eventual brilliance even before they began their intelligence generating program. One of them, Pastor Witte, declared in 1800, even before his child was born:

If God grants me a son, and if he, in your opinion, is not to be called stupid, which Heaven forbid, I have long ago decided to educate him to be a superior man, without knowing in advance what his aptitudes may be. *

Pastor Witte initiated a program of vocabulary expansion for his son, Karl, even before the child could walk, and pursued a program of reading instruction soon after. The youngster entered the University of Leipzig at age nine and had his Ph.D. at thirteen.

One hundred and fifty-two years later, Aaron Stern stated that he didn't intend his newborn daughter Edith to be merely a normal child, but rather a superior human being. In Stern's words,

When I invited friends to see [the infant] I told them bluntly that she was

---

* Pastor Witte, *The Education of Karl Witte or The Training of the Child* (Arno Press, originally published 1914).

** Aaron Stern, *The Making of a Genius* (Renaissance Publications, 1971).

destined to become "a genius."**

Daughter Edith was reading before age two. She entered college at the age of twelve and was teaching mathematics at Michigan State University by the time she was fifteen.

With such well publicized predictions, and fulfilments, of intellectual advancement resulting wholly or largely from early literacy, workers at the Institutes had no cause for surprise at the influence early reading has on the brain. No, their biggest surprise — and it was a blockbuster — came when they noticed that the intelligence of children with half- or diseased brains rose under the effects of intellectual stimulation not merely to a normal level, but even *higher* than that of normal children. At this point, the stunned experimenters began to wonder what was wrong with normal children.

They concluded that the only thing "wrong" with normal children is that their perfectly healthy, potentially powerful, undamaged brains are seldom confronted with the need for complicated thought. But if we enrich children's intellectual menus, we promote the emergence of intellectually superior beings.

A colleague of mine in Ottawa supplied interesting anecdotal evidence when he related the following story.

Some years back, he and his family were in the process of moving. Their household effects were in storage. With time on her hands, my friend's wife — who had never taught children before — decided to teach their twenty-one-month-old son John to read. Why would anyone want to teach a child this young to read? The mother merely wanted to let the youngster begin enjoying books.

Because their books were in storage, the only reading material at hand was, of all things, a liquor price list. So the infant learned phonics with such words as *rum, vodka, port,* and so on. Soon, however, the youngster graduated to non-alcoholic reading (and you may be happy to know that the adult John — now a professor of economics — isn't a booze-hound). By the time the boy entered grade 1, he had read about 250 books.

His parents hadn't considered what effect early reading might have on their son's eventual school performance. The matter hadn't crossed their minds for the simple reason that they weren't aware any connection existed between the two. Nevertheless, when John eventually attended school, he brought home so many cups and awards for scholarly achievement that they had to be kept in boxes in the basement. In college he secured the highest mark ever given for a graduation thesis in honors economics.

John's parents didn't presume to be scholars, nor were they academically inclined. In consequence, they never became major contributors to his continuing education. Early reading instruction was *the only instruction* John ever received at home. John's younger sister, Kathryn, also taught to read at an early age, attained genius-level intelligence and enjoyed an equally spectacular school record.

I had an incidental chance to note the connection between early reading ability and advanced intelligence. A number of years ago, before I founded the Institute, I was invited to address a group of ten- and eleven-year-olds — about thirty youngsters altogether — who were engaged in a program for children with genius intelligence (having IQs of 140 or higher). At the end of my talk (which happened to deal with writing, not intellectual performance) I asked the youngsters how many of them had been able to read when they began school. Every hand shot up.

But wait — which came first, the chicken or the egg? Does early reading ability promote high intelligence or were all the previously mentioned bright children reading early only because they were bright?

The record shows that children read early if, and only if, they are taught to read, and that those who are not taught — though they may be brilliant — will remain illiterate. Additional evidence supports the belief that if other factors in a child's life don't favor or promote high intelligence, early reading ability provides a powerful boost.

A normal child is born with a data-processing device of amazing power — the human brain. Yet, for most children, their brains are seldom offered the stimulation of complicated thought. TV cartoons, video games, sports, and small talk conducted in low-count vocabularies provide low-nutrient soil for intellectual growth.

But introduce reading, and everything changes. Reading gives children access to rich, previously untapped sources of information — the printed words that surround them. Additionally, the brute mechanics of the reading process demand neural effort. Consider this: reading requires the decipherment of a code — an intricate system of squiggles and their many permutations that must first be translated into sound, then to thought. This is the stuff that makes synapses snap, crackle, and pop. This is cerebral trampolining. This is thought processing at its finest. This is the activity that promotes brain growth.

Yes, growth — for, though the brain isn't a muscle, it responds to exercise exactly as a muscle does. Studies conducted at the University of California at Berkeley by Dr. Mark Rosenzweig and others showed that when a brain is pressed into greater use, it exhibits both physical and chemical changes. Burdened with a heavier workload, the brain grows more receptor spines per unit-length of dendrite, and cells develop a higher content of ribonucleic acid.

We're not talking here about *maybe* or *perhaps*. We're talking about documented proof arising from research conducted by respected scientists. And we're talking about changes *you* can make in your own child's thought circuitry with just a little effort.

Reading is not, of course, the only propellant of thinking and of heightened intelligence. Those who test intelligence report an intimate link between size of vocabulary and intelligence. They find that a child's score on the vocabulary portion of an IQ test is about the same as the child's score on the entire test.

"Boy wonder" of the theater world, Orson Welles, didn't read early, but the unusual instruction he received, while still an infant, in other intellect-building matters — notably speech and vocabulary enrichment — enabled him to remark that "the desire to take medicine is one of the greatest features which distinguish men from animals," at age *eighteen months*. And consider two other children, George and Woodrow, who didn't learn to read until they were ages eleven and twelve respectively. However, their parents were well educated, so, like Welles, the youngsters gained an unusually rich early speech vocabulary; and this, we might assume, is what saved General George S. Patton and Woodrow Wilson from obscurity.*

---

* One might wonder, though, whether so late a start in reading is the principal reason General Patton never became a skilful reader.

No wonder the famous McGuffey readers packed such an intelligence-lifting wallop. The readers, first published in 1837 (and still in print), combined the two powerful intelligence-generating forces: reading instruction and vocabulary enrichment. Consider, for example, a report on elephants in the *McGuffey Fourth Reader*, which employs the words *quadruped, pendulous, proboscis, stratagem, docile, unwieldy*, and *tacitly*, and provides definitions for each. Not surprisingly, this blend of advanced reading and vocabulary enrichment created a rare and potent force for social mobility, permitting the children of uneducated immigrant families to compete academically and intellectually with children from better-endowed homes. While immigrant mothers hunched over sweatshop sewing machines and fathers labored in ditches, their primary-school children gained from the six McGuffey readers not only sharp minds, but a command of English possessed by few university graduates today. This was an intellectual and academic boon that won them easy access to the social, professional, and corporate ladders, and a prompt ascendancy thereof.

Admittedly, not every highly intelligent person was an early reader or the possessor of an exceptionally rich vocabulary. However, the evidence seems to show that, in the absence of other intelligence-promoting influences — of which there are several — learning to read generates its own special whirlwind of cerebral stimulation.

Almost three hundred years ago, Joseph Addison, statesman and man of letters, said, "Reading is to the mind what exercise is to the body." Little did he imagine that measurements of brain cells would one day prove his metaphorical assertion to be physiologically true.

The surge in brain power predicted by the University of California studies seemed to be substantiated by a neighbor of mine. Her son, Peter, had been born with a grossly misshapen head and the child's performance in his early years indicated brain damage. At age four, Peter could barely walk and easily lost his balance. His speech was so garbled his mother alone could understand what he was trying to say.

To advance the lad's physical ability, his mother bought Lego so he could learn and practise the pincer grip. Then she tied his feet to the pedals of a pedal-cart and pushed him along, in time reducing her pushing (without his knowing) until he was propelling himself. She spent six hours a day teaching him to recite nursery rhymes, and then began teaching him to read. By the time the youngster was six, he could read simple sentences and count to one hundred.

Having moved to another city, where no one knew of the child's early handicap, the mother entered him in a grade 1 program. His teacher soon reported that Peter was brilliant, and enriched his work. Three years later, when Peter was in grade 4, the principal wanted to promote the "genius child" to grade 6.

This single report isn't admissible as scientific proof. Such would require a quantity of like successes, carefully monitored. However, similar cases are difficult to unearth, not because they don't exist (I have heard whispers of others), but because when parents have "normalized" a retarded child they don't want it known that he or she was ever less than apple-cheeked normal.

The seeming assurance of intellectual growth is therefore a crowning reason for teaching a young child to read. It is remarkable, and regrettable, considering this and the other excellent reasons for early instruction, that most youngsters are denied the opportunity to begin reading until they are six or seven.

DOES ALL THIS EMPHASIS ON EARLY READING INSTRUCTION MEAN SCHOOL-AGE CHILDREN HAVE MISSED THE BRAIN BOAT?

According to a highly respected researcher in early-childhood studies — and you may want to sit down for this — about fifty percent of our intellectual development has been fixed by age four, and eighty percent of it by age eight.

How powerful was your thinking at age four? And at age eight? The researcher's findings would seem to mean that the Divine Exchequer quietly amortized our brain-power during childhood on a short-term non-renegotiable plan, which dooms us to stumble through life in our present less-than-perfect state.

But wait, before we reach for the Valium, could an error have been made somewhere? Fortunately, yes. Further studies of brain tissue at the University of California show neurons (brain cells) retain a plasticity — an almost magical potential for renewed growth. This regenerative ability extends into old age and permits the brain to change in structure and in power if it is obliged to bear a heavier intellectual load.

Please note, I am not saying that one whose thinking has been honed by putting the red lids on the red tins and the striped lids on the striped tins is suddenly going to burst forth and lead a nation (though, on second thought, perhaps it's already happened). I submit only that when the brain is obliged to begin dealing with complex matters, it will gradually acquire the necessary power to do so. This new power will be comparable to what the brain could have secured earlier in life.

It is the constancy or permanency of the prevailing richness (or poverty) of an environment — not age — that encourages a rise (or fall) in intelligence. Dull company promotes dullness in one's own thinking. A child grows up in an environment of fixed intellectual worth. The child's intelligence grows to fit the intellectual mold of that environment, only to be eventually imprisoned by it. But change the child's environment, or introduce thought-nutrients, and brain growth begins anew; regeneration proceeds.

Reading provides a particularly powerful form of nutrient. The decoding ritual of the phonic method entails the same cerebral exercise for a six- or seven-year-old as it does for a two- or three-year-old. Moreover, a child who reads can escape via books to an intellectually richer environment populated by interesting and knowledgeable people, both fictional and real.

DO I HAVE TO KNOW ANYTHING ABOUT TEACHING CHILDREN?

Despite the assurances that have already been given concerning the ease with which children can be taught to read, this question remains foremost in parents' minds.

The answer is an emphatic "No!" Parents are usually astonished when they discover how easily children can be taught to read — as I was astonished when I began teaching my own children. At that time I wasn't in education, had never taught children before, knew nothing about reading instruction, and had no book to guide me.

The reading program we will be using — a program much improved over the one I created in 1972 — is essentially the same one used at the Institute today. However, you have an advantage over my teachers. Because children enter our program at various times throughout the year (often, in the junior room, as soon as they are toilet-trained), children in the same class are usually reading at different levels. With twelve youngsters to guide and instruct, our teachers can give only ten minutes of individual reading instruction per day to each child: five minutes in the morning and five minutes in the afternoon. You, on the other hand, can give fifteen or twenty minutes of individual instruction to your child each day, if you wish. And because the program is fun, your pupil may urge you to do so. In that case, he or she will advance all the more quickly.

WHAT IF I JUST DON'T HAVE THE TIME OR THE PATIENCE TO TEACH?

Some parents, lacking time, patience, or confidence, may welcome the part-time or full-time help of a teaching assistant. Even if you don't want help at the beginning of your program, you may later. In fact, an occasional change of teacher can regenerate a child's interest if it ever wanes (though techniques are described in later chapters to make your program maximally entertaining). Ways to find excellent low-cost tutors are described in chapter 4.

WHY NOT LEAVE READING INSTRUCTION TO THE PROFESSIONALS TEACHING GRADE 1?

This is a popular question, one with several answers.

First, teaching a preschooler to read is so simple that there isn't any justification for delaying the task until grade 1. After all, parents don't delay teaching their children to speak until grade 1. Yet, learning to speak — which normally takes a year or two — is a far more difficult venture for a child than learning to read. As the celebrated mathematician and philosopher Alfred North Whitehead noted, "What an appalling task, the correlation of meaning with sounds." Speech is difficult. Reading is easy by comparison — when an easy program of instruction is used.

Second, the preschooler who can read gains the several important advantages discussed earlier.

Third, leaving a child's reading instruction to the public school system can be risky. The task of teaching thirty or more children — all with varying speech ability, varying intelligence, and varying interest in any form of learning — is burden enough for schoolteachers. Yet the burden is often made heavier by the need for behavior modification: teaching children to sit still, pay attention, listen, and be quiet — a continuing daily task for teachers that doesn't favor quick reading progress for anyone.

Also, teachers are not always taught what is essential and what is unessential to ensure quick literacy. Consider the common practice of teaching children the alphabet, a procedure carried out in almost every kindergarten and grade 1 classroom.

Teaching children the *names* of the letters — *ay, bee, see, dee, ee, eff, jee,* and so on — has no value when teaching children to read. In fact, knowing the names of the letters can confuse children and slow learning when they are asked to forget *ay, bee, see* and instead learn the *sounds* of the letters. This classic misconception persists in classrooms today because teachers long ago were convinced that skill in naming the letters guaranteed children's quick reading progress. Teachers in ancient Greece obliged their pupils to recite the alphabet from alpha through to omega (the equivalent of our A, B, C, through to Z). Then, to make doubly sure the children would advance quickly in reading, they compelled them to recite the alphabet backwards, from omega to alpha (in our alphabet, Z, Y, X, through to A).

British teachers were still perpetuating this lapse of logic centuries later, and if, after this sure-fire instruction schoolchildren persisted in reading poorly, they were flogged for obstinacy. This gruesome performance seems painfully amusing today, yet the practice endures like bubble gum under a school desk in most kindergarten and grade 1 classrooms. Now, of course, flogging is out, and children are obliged to chant the alphabet only one way, from A to Z. So, we progress.

Knowing the *names* of the letters — reciting the alphabet — is of no value, none whatsoever, in teaching children to read. Knowing these letter names is important only when we teach children to spell. But spelling is best shelved until we get children reading skilfully.

Teachers are also handicapped by the misdirection they are given by publishers of poorly devised reading programs — and there are plenty in use. You may wonder how faulty reading programs could be foisted upon school boards. Attribute it to glitz, a veneer of high-tech know-how, clever marketing, and the fact that those who control school board purchasing have probably never taught a child to read. The bureaucratic befuddlement that impedes improvement in public schooling is detailed in chapter 6.

Such are the hazards that could prevent your child from becoming a skilful, enthusiastic reader in a public school. There are, of course, some teachers who, using a purely phonic reading program, never fail to graduate a class of excellent readers. Such teachers, though, are in the minority. Consequently, the unfortunate bottom line is that *the only child who is guaranteed to be reading skilfully on completing grade 1 is the child who was reading skilfully on entering grade 1.*

Parents of all other children are gambling, though they seldom realize it. Many lose their bets — and we meet them and hear their sad stories at our remedial reading clinics.

The fourth and final reason for not leaving your child's reading instruction to professionals is simply that the gift of literacy is too wonderful to be left for its giving solely to those outside a child's family. This is why my teachers encourage parents to participate in their child's reading advancement and provide materials so they may do so. Of all the wondrous delights you may confer upon your child, few will match the enduring pleasure that literacy provides.

CAN ALL TWO- AND THREE-YEAR-OLDS LEARN TO READ?

Any preschooler able to speak can be taught to read. The limiting factor, if there be one, will be determined by the specific child, the parent, and the established relationship between the two. First, let's consider the child.

Maturity is more important than age. Some two-year-olds are further advanced in manner and speech than other children age three, so there's no simple answer to how quickly this particular two-year-old or that three-year-old will respond to reading instruction.

Next, the parent. With the program presented here, neither previous knowledge nor experience is needed to teach a preschooler to read. What is needed instead is a readiness to put aside preconceived ideas about how you *think* a child should learn. Children don't learn the same way adults do. For example, if you were to explain something to an adult, and find the next day that he had forgotten the matter, you would patiently explain the detail again. But if on the next day he had forgotten once again, you might wonder about his intelligence.

Such judgment is inappropriate when working with young children. A preschooler may forget something ten or twenty times — and, even more mystifyingly, correctly follow a procedure a hundred times, then suddenly forget. This doesn't mean there is anything wrong with the child. It means you and I have an imperfect understanding of how very young minds learn to deal with our complicated world.

Finally, the relationship between parent and child is important. Winning a child's cooperation in some playful activity is, for most parents, simplicity itself. For these parents, the fun and nonsense generated by the reading games presented later will provide many pleasurable moments, made all the more memorable by their child's rapid reading progress.

Some parents, though, may lack confidence in their teaching ability, or may have difficulty holding their child's attention, or may be pressed for time. Helpful hints are included to deal with these difficulties.

CAN TWO- AND THREE-YEAR-OLDS UNDERSTAND THE WORDS THEY ARE READING?

Children can understand in print those words — and *only* those words — they understand in speech, the same limitation that applies to adults. And because young children have such a small speech vocabulary, we must teach them the meaning of new words while we are teaching them to read. Fittingly, our program begins with simple words that two-year-olds either know or can easily be taught.

IF A CHILD CAN READ ON ENTERING SCHOOL, WON'T THE CHILD BE BORED?

There is little reason for a child to be bored in school simply because he or she can read. In most grade 1 classrooms, much of the day is given over to matters that appeal to all children. The atmosphere is often club-like, and peer relationship and social skills get a lot of attention. There might be morning exercises, health, safety, art, nature studies, crafts, videos, show and tell, story time, game time, music, and any number of other activities the teacher thinks important.

On the other hand, if a child enters a grade 1 classroom where the emphasis is on reading, printing, and arithmetic (bearing in mind that no two grade 1 classrooms are identical), the teacher might divide the class into groups. The advanced children (the readers) will form their own group, average children will form another, and children needing special attention will form a third. It is these last children who are most vulnerable to boredom; finding the work difficult, they often fall behind and lose interest.

There are several reasons why children might be bored in school, but children who can read probably have less reason than others for being bored. They can read books while their classmates are learning how to (possibly by a difficult and confusing method). And if the advanced children ever find the work unchallenging, the teacher can give them enrichment materials.

But let's suppose — let's just suppose — that a reading child draws a grade 1 teacher too lacking in spirit to provide stimulating work for the youngster. Would we want to withhold a child's preschool education and intellectual advancement simply so he or she will fit in comfortably with a worst-case scenario teacher? If the teacher is too lacking in enterprise to deal appropriately with a child who can already read, it may be a tedious and unproductive year for the entire class.

There is good reason, on the other hand, for a grade 1 teacher to be delighted when a reading child enters her class. Each such child is counted at the end of the year among the teacher's reading successes — an automatic win for the teacher. Pass Go. Collect $200.

Chapter 7 describes ways to help ensure your early reader's easy acceptance of, and adjustment to, a public school program (though you might consider continuing your child's education wholly at home — an increasingly common practice).

WON'T CHILDREN TEACH THEMSELVES TO READ WHEN THEY ARE READY?

This hopeful sentiment, expressed from time to time by one or another educator, has prompted some parents to sit back and wait for the event to happen. However, studies show that children who reputedly taught themselves to read had a special aptitude for learning to read, but they did *not,* in fact, teach themselves.

Some children find that reading comes easily to them, just as some eventually discover that math comes easily to them. A few clues are enough to help them begin puzzling out the procedures that grant literacy. For example, simply moving a finger beneath the words while reading to a child on one's lap is enough to teach some children one of the first rules of reading: that it progresses from left to right along a line, then drops to the line immediately below and continues again from left to right. Not all children will pick this up immediately — just some with minds disposed to such observation. Similarly, if a parent reads the same story several times to such a child, the youngster can acquire a "sight-word" vocabulary by noting the distinctive overall appearance of certain words (capitalizing on what are termed in educational circles *configuration clues*).

Given this much unintentioned guidance, plus answers to their questions — from either an adult or another child (perhaps even by playing school with an older child) — some children begin to see the connection between letters and sounds. They then begin cracking the letter-sound code, and are soon figuring out simple words on their own. But the fact that by happy accident a few favored children can puzzle out the basic reading procedures on their own is no reason to avoid giving *your* child all the help you can.

In short, children described as self-taught are the special few who are favorably disposed to begin reading with minimal *unrecognized instruction*, and who receive that inadvertent help.

Of the several matters that have been discussed in this chapter, the most important are:

1. Teaching a preschooler to read is both easy and advisable.
2. Equipping children of any age with the means to read and enjoy books on their own is only the immediately visible benefit of literacy. The more profound benefit is the intellectual advancement generated in the process.

Think, then, of the truly priceless advantages you are in a position to give your child with just a few minutes of your time each day. This book is dedicated to helping you do that.

If we regard the price you paid for this book as a tuition fee — and why not? — might we then consider your child as being a member of the extended student body of the Sidney Ledson Institute for Intellectual Advancement? If so, may I figuratively extend a hand out from the page and suggest we proceed, as partners, to give your child or children the wonderful gift of literacy and heightened intelligence.

HOW DO I GET STARTED?

Chapter 2 is the key to the entire reading program. It gives, in a step-by-step manner, detailed basic information needed for you to begin your own teaching program. When you have read chapter 2 — or whatever portion of it you immediately opt for (there is a choice) — you will be able to start your program as soon as you wish.

2

The First
100 Words

Learning to ride a bicycle is about equally difficult for a pre-schooler, a schoolchild, and an adult. Steering, balance, and pedalling must be mastered by all. In a similar way, learning to read obliges learners of every age to master identical rules. There isn't any special method for adults that differs from one for schoolchildren that in turn differs from one suitable for preschoolers. All must learn the business of assigning sounds to letters.

The reading program in this book was created to the specifications of two-year-olds, but that doesn't make the system unsuitable for teaching anyone older than two. Quite to the contrary, the simplified method assures learners of all ages quicker reading advancement than was ever before possible.

This chapter is a "nuts and bolts" presentation designed to teach you how to teach reading with the phonic method. The information given here is meant to serve as a constant reference for you as you proceed with your particular teaching goal, as further discussed in chapters 3 through 7. For example, if you are planning to teach a preschooler, this present chapter will serve as a companion piece to the information given in chapter 3: "Teaching a Preschooler." However, if you are a kindergarten or grade 1 teacher, the information given here is meant to accompany the instructions given in chapter 6: "Kindergarten and Grade 1 Teachers." The same marriage of information holds for all others whose teaching goals are dealt with later in specific chapters.

When you have read as far as step 4, you can either continue reading the rest of this chapter or begin teaching your pupil or pupils, using the techniques given in the chapter devoted to your specific purpose.

Because this reading program was designed to include two-year-olds, the first words taught in the program are ones that two-year-olds know or can easily be taught (though we will be expanding this infant vocabulary). And because short words are easier to read than long words, we will begin with one of the shortest words in our language: *UP*, concentrating first on the letters *U* and *P* rather than on the complete word.

To begin teaching the word *UP*, you must be able to sound *U* and *P* correctly. Before you can do this, I must convey to you the correct sound to be assigned to each. Therein lies a major problem, because some sounds can be difficult to convey in printed form. For example, we can all identify the sound of a siren, a telephone ring, and a bird song, but how might we represent these same sounds in print so that a person who hasn't heard them before can get a clear understanding of each? To illustrate, what's this?: z-z-z-z-z-z-z. Give up? It's the sound a vacuum cleaner makes. You didn't stand a chance, did you? I hope to do better in describing the sounds we give to letters of the alphabet, though it may be a challenge for both of us: my ability, and your patience.

If I seem to dwell overly long on the task of interpreting letter sounds, it is because my experience in training teachers at the Institute has proven the process to be harder than it seems. Before prospective teachers begin our training program, they receive a tape cassette on which the first fifteen letter sounds are correctly made. They take the tape home, listen to it a few times, and learn to mimic the sounds. Simple? So it would seem. Yet, on testing trainees the next day, we find they invariably make mistakes. Corrected, they listen to the tape that night, practise the sounds, and try again the next day — and, as often as not, they still make mistakes. You don't have the tape cassette to help you, so please proceed carefully in learning the letter sounds. Some people will be able to make the sounds easily and correctly and will wonder what the fuss is all about. But we find that most people will say, "Hey, nothing to it," and then get them *wrong.*

It's worth taking extra time to learn the sounds correctly because the more accurately you can sound the letters, the more easily your child or children will progress.

Use of the word *letter* to indicate the various designs and squiggles that make up our alphabet is unfortunate, for it gives no hint of the job these squiggles perform. *Sound symbol* is a better term and it's one we will use interchangeably with *letter.*

We all know that the sound of some letters or sound symbols is different in different words — as, for example, the *U* in *cut* and *cute.* However, these changes in sound conform to well established and commonly understood rules. Still, we don't want to burden learners with rules until they have gained some elementary reading ability. When children have learned the sound values of individual letters, we can then begin teaching them new sounds that are conveyed by combinations of letters — as, for example the *OA* in *road*, the *AY* in *play*, the *EW* in *few*, and so on.

There are, of course, a number of words that don't conform to simple rules of pronunciation: *who, canoe, viscount, yacht, magician,* and so on, but these and other exceptions are easily taught when the need arises.

Sans serif letters

From this point on, letters and words being taught will be shown in sans serif letters. This will serve to remind you that the letters and words you print for your pupil should also be without serifs. If you are unfamiliar with the term *serif*, it refers to the small projections at the ends of the strokes of some letters. The following two sentences will illustrate.

THIS SERIES OF WORDS SHOWS LETTERS WITH SERIFS.
THIS SERIES OF WORDS SHOWS LETTERS WITHOUT SERIFS.

THE 32 STEPS

Step 1: U

The first sound to learn is the sound we give to the letter **U** — which happens to be an easy one. Everyone knows that the name of this letter sounds like *yoo*. Please forget *yoo* for the moment. In fact, forget *yoo* and all the other letter names until that later date when you begin teaching your child to print and spell. As explained in chapter 1, we are not interested in teaching letter names. It not only wastes time, it eventually confuses the learner. The sound to associate with the symbol **U** in your pupil's mind is reasonably well conveyed by the letters **uh**. Here is how to make the sound correctly.

Pretend you are playing the part of a Mugaboo warrior in a movie. You have a talking part — or, more accurately, a grunting part. When the hero eyes your daughter, you are supposed to grunt. And because you want to make the most of your one-grunt message, you make it a long **u-u-uh**. And if, while doing this, you stretch the sides of your mouth out and down, not only will the director be impressed, but you'll be making the exact sound we want your child to associate with the sound symbol **U**.

If your pupil has, unfortunately, already learned to associate the sound *yoo* with **U**, you can explain that *yoo* is the *name* of the letter, not its sound. Just as you might say *cow* is the name of the animal, but not its sound, which happens to be *moo*.

Step 2: P

The next sound symbol you will be teaching your pupil is **P**, which is normally called *pee*. Please forget *pee*. The sound we want your learner to associate with this shape is poorly represented (remember the vacuum cleaner?) by the letters *Puh*. What makes this representation of the sound so misleading is that we have just finished learning for the letter **U** that **uh** is a grunt, which is a *voiced* sound, meaning one in which the vocal chords vibrate. However, the *uh* in *Puh* is *not* voiced.

To help you determine whether to use your voice when sounding letters, they will be shown in bold — **uh** — when the voice is to be used, and not — *uh* — when the voice is not used.

The sound we want for *Puh* is merely a blast of air as the lips part. There is no grunt or groan at any time — either before, during, or after the lips separate. It is a quiet sound. In fact, if the sound is properly made it can't be heard several feet away. To check your performance in sounding the letter correctly, place your hand on your throat. If your vocal chords vibrate at any time, you are making the sound incorrectly. No voice. No grunt. Just pucker your lips and release a small explosion of air.

Because our teacher trainees have so much difficulty sounding this letter correctly, let's go over it again. Suppose a fly is stuck in the mustard on your hot dog. You pucker your lips, build up air pressure in your mouth, then launch the fly out of the mustard with a blast of air. In so doing, you make the correct sound for **P**. No voice, no groan — just air.

The letter **P** is one of seven voiceless letters (**C**, **F**, **H**, **K**, **S**, and **T** being the others) to which we will be giving special attention. To better understand the difference between voiced and unvoiced sounds, consider that there are two ways to whisper. One way is to speak very quietly, using your voice as you normally would. The other way — a "safer" whisper you might have used in school — is the hissed whisper. The voice isn't used at all. There is no vibration in your throat. Words are formed by the mouth and tongue in the usual way, and the flow of escaping air does the rest.

P, then, is the first of seven voiceless letter sounds we will be examining. Master the sound of **P**, and the others will be easier to learn. You might record your expression of **P** on a tape recorder, then compare that sound to the description above.

Step 3: UP

Having learned **U** and **P**, your pupil is ready to read the first word, **UP**. But first, you may be wondering why we teach children to read in capital letters rather than lower-case or "small" letters. There are two reasons. First, some of the earliest opportunities for beginning readers to use their newly acquired reading skill are when they see street signs, company names, car names, and advertising captions, all of which are usually printed in capital letters.

The second reason has to do with *configuration clues*: a technique used to help children who haven't been taught the letter sounds (or, if taught the letter sounds, haven't been adequately exercised in using them). *Configuration clues, context clues,* and *picture clues* make up what are known as *word attack skills* — a collection of tricks that often promote guessing instead of reading.

Configuration means "shape," and in this instance it refers to the overall shape of a word. To illustrate: the first two words in our reading program are **UP** and **CUP**. Printed in lower-case letters — **up** and **cup** — the two words take on distinctive shapes that could help a child distinguish between them if he or she weren't able to puzzle them out solely by the sounds of their letters.

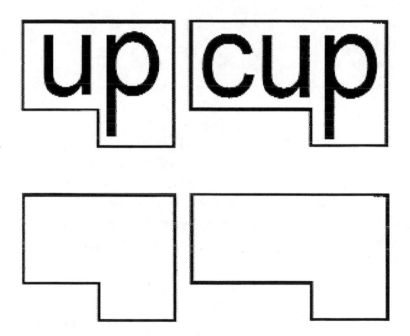

Figure 1: Configurations as reading clues

By teaching children words printed in capital letters — which are uniform in height and have no projecting components to their shape — we oblige learners to rely solely on their knowledge of letters and letter sounds. Such is the no-fail, non-guessing route to skilful reading.

Back to our program.

In teaching the word **UP**, we are teaching children much more than how to read a word. We are teaching them a system — one that, yes, permits the reading of **UP**, but, more importantly, leads to the reading of all other words the children (and the eventual adults) will ever read.

The first rule in the system, as you have seen, is that letters must be sounded. The second rule is that we always start sounding on the left side, and never on the right. By continually reinforcing this left-to-right procedure (though without using the words *left* and *right* if your pupil isn't familiar with the terms), we reduce the chance of a learner ever reading backwards. There may be slip-ups from time to time, but errors will diminish as your pupil gains experience in reading.

The matter of blending

We seldom realize that, in speaking, we utter a rapid succession of individual sounds blended together to form "word packets." This detail is further obscured by the fact that the word packets are then quickly blended together to form sentence packets. But if we examine just a single word — say, *fun* — we get a clearer picture of the speech process.

When we say "fun", the word comes out as a single blast of sound, one with an ill-defined division of sounds. But if we record this word, then play it back at a fraction of its recorded speed, we will hear *f-f-f-f-f-u-u-u-u-u-n-n-n-n-n*. Perhaps you have heard speech slowed to this extent, slowed so much that consonants and vowels become separated, making words difficult to understand. That is the same problem children face when they begin sounding individual letters in an effort to identify a word. By the time the learner has sounded *uh*, then ***P****uh* — which might take two seconds — the letter sounds have become too loosely linked for the child to recognize them as being the components of **UP**. Of course, we can draw attention to this detail and utter the sounds more quickly to provide a clue, but children usually have to grasp this processing technique on their own and at their own comfortable speed.

Seeing the task now from the learner's viewpoint, you will understand the need for patience. Don't concern yourself if your child doesn't immediately see any connection between *uh* and ***P****uh*. There's no hurry. You may, of course, help your youngster see the connection by asking him or her to speak the appropriate word after sounding its letters. The child will do this to humor you, probably without seeing the connection. Not to worry; after reading a hundred words or so, the child will gradually acquire the ability to identify words from their detached sound parts.

Perhaps it has occurred to you that knowing how to sound **U** and **P** permits the reading of a second word — **PUP**. True, and how quickly you include this second word will depend on the maturity of your learner.

The golden rule of teaching

Never, *never* move ahead with material while your learner is still unsure about what has already been taught. Nothing slows learning as much as confusion. Confidence plummets. Tension mounts. Thinking is clouded. A young child may need a week to attach the correct sound to **U**, and another week for **P**. Don't worry if progress seems slow. The child is learning important details: first, that a specific sound is called for on seeing a specific shape, and second, that shapes are sounded from left to right — two monumental steps forward. Be patient.

Decision

You have now learned enough to begin your teaching program. You might, therefore, want to turn to the chapter that deals with your particular teaching goal, or you may prefer to continue reading this chapter and preview the ways in which your reading program will pick up speed. Those whose goal is other than that of teaching a preschooler — dealt with in chapter 3 — will nevertheless find valuable guidance in that chapter that they can transfer to their own special task.

Step 4: C

The next sound to be learned is the one associated with the letter **C** — which everyone calls *see*. Please forget *see*. The sound we want your pupil to associate with this letter shape is one that, like *Puh*, is voiceless: another of our hissed-whisper group. No voice, no grunt — just air.

In case the description of the sound for *Puh* was inadequate, let's go through *Cuh* in detail, and, by doing, perhaps improve the chances of both *Puh* and *Cuh* being accurately expressed. Back to the movie set.

In reality, you weren't a Mugaboo warrior at all, but a world-class scientist on a secret mission. Now, however, you are trussed to a chair and the bad guys are playing poker a few feet away behind a curtain. Beside you, similarly trussed, is a singing greeting-card messenger. (Boy, did *he* pick the wrong address!) You have both wriggled free from your bonds and are planning to escape out the window. In case you get shot, you hiss the secret formula that has to be delivered to the good guys. Unfortunately, you stutter.

"Three c-c-capsules of c-c-chlorine, a k-k-kilo of c-c-carbon, and a c-c-cup of c-c-caramel c-c-custard."

As long as you remember to use a hissed whisper for this short vital message, you will make the correct sound for the letter **C** several times. Or, you might try it in slow motion: close the throat passage with the back part of your tongue, then quickly remove the tongue to release a small burst of air. Correctly made, the sound doesn't travel far because there is no voiced component. Remember that the *uh* in *Cuh* means no voice, no grunt — just air.

Step 5: CUP

When your pupil has learned to correctly express the sound for *Cuh* (which could take a week for a very young child), you can then teach the third word in our program: **CUP**.

Remember to encourage your pupil to sound each letter aloud before identifying the word (perhaps with your help). And reinforce the left-to-right sounding-out procedure. These two important points merit additional comment.

Uttering and fingering

Never discourage your pupil from sounding aloud the individual letters before identifying a word. Indeed, even if your learner shows skill in identifying words *without* sounding their letters, insist that the letters be sounded. At this stage we want a learner to voice the letter sounds aloud hundreds of times. By so doing, the child will gain sufficient familiarity with each letter sound to eventually be able to process them silently, mentally, automatically, and quickly, as you and I do.

Additionally, don't discourage your pupil from tracing a finger beneath each letter being sounded. The coordination of muscles required by this action helps to fix the important left-to-right procedure more securely in a child's mind. When, eventually, your youngster no longer feels the need to trace a finger — perhaps after having read several hundred words — he or she will discontinue the practice. But don't rush it.

Sounds of word beginnings

Tunnels are more quickly dug when digging proceeds from both ends. Similarly, your pupil will more quickly see the connection between letter sounds and entire words if he or she is sensitized to the fact that a spoken word is divisible into smaller, detectable and distinguishable sound units. And, of these, the sound most easily isolated from the rest of a spoken word is its beginning sound. So, during odd moments — not necessarily during your regular reading sessions — help your child detect the beginning sound of various words by voicing them with a stutter: "What sound does *u-u-u-up* start with, Sebastian?"

Don't expect your pupil to immediately detect the beginning sound. The idea that spoken words have smaller aural units is a startling notion to the young learner. Proceed with others: *u-u-u-umbrella, u-u-u-uncle, u-u-u-us,* and *u-u-u-umpire* (if the child knows what an umpire is) If you ask the same questions, in the same manner, two or three times a day, your pupil will begin to see what you are getting at, and will provide the appropriate answer (taking a longer or shorter time to do so depending on the child's age and maturity).

In that **P** doesn't immediately fill a beginning-sound role in our program, skip it and proceed with **C**. "What sound does *c-c-c-cup* start with, Gloriana-Lee?" Proceed similarly with other words that begin with **C**.

Avoid using the word *word*, as in the question, "What does the word *u-u-u-upstairs* start with?" *Word* may have no more meaning for the youngster than *adjective* or *adverb*, and your learner would be confused before you had finished asking the question. Always bear this general caution in mind.

When quizzing your child or explaining any matter, be careful you don't use words or expressions the youngster may not know. If you ask a two-year-old, "What sound does *cat* start with?" he or she may be baffled by simply not knowing the meanings of the word *sound* or the expression *start with*. If the child is unsure of terms such as this, give some time to vocabulary growth before proceeding with your reading program.

Step 6: A

Introduce the sound-symbol **A**, which is usually voiced *ay*. Please forget *ay*. The sound we want your pupil to attach to this letter can't be shown symbolically, so I'll describe it. If you say the words *hat, sat,* and *cat*, the sound in the middle of each word is the sound we want your pupil to learn. (But don't mention *hat, sat,* or *cat* to your child. These examples are for *your* instruction, not your pupil's.)

A — the second vowel to be learned — invites a word of caution. The sounds of the vowels — **A, E, I, O,** and **U** — *if mumbled,* sound almost alike to the undiscriminating ear of a young child. For this reason, we tell teacher trainees to stretch their mouths to the maximum in whatever position is required to produce the most distinctive sound for each vowel. For **A** (and remember, forget *ay*), stretch your mouth sideways as far as you can, drop the corners slightly, let the tongue lie flat, and voice a nice flat **A** — the same sound heard in the word *flat*.

Step 7: CAP

We can now add **CAP** to your pupil's reading list.

Step 8: T

The next sound-symbol, **T** — which we will show as *Tuh* — is another hissed sound, not the voiced *tee*. Please forget *tee*. Remember the hissed appeal you made to your fellow captive in the film? Actually, he was a counter-intelligence triple agent in disguise. He has slipped his bonds and is now trying to defuse an explosive device, an act made all the more difficult because he has lost his glasses. You whisper to him (with the *hissed* whisper), "Don't t-t-tinker with the t-t-time-bomb,

T-T-Terence." In hissing this salubrious advice, you expertly express the correct sound for **T** several times.

My resort to outrageous drama — which might raise some readers' spirit — is meant to entice you to mimic the hissed message and, by so doing, gain a better understanding of the required sound. Try it.

When sounded correctly, *Tuh* — like *Puh* and *Cuh* — will not be heard more than a few feet away, which can present a problem for schoolteachers hoping to be heard at the back of the classroom. But don't give the sound a voiced accompaniment to extend its audible reach. Just move rearward.

Step 9: Words using T

With *Tuh* now learned, your pupil is ready to read the words **AT**, **PAT**, **CAT**, **TAP**, and **CUT**. Technically, the word *put* might be included, but the *U* in *put* conveys a sound different from the sound your pupil recently learned for this letter, and we don't want to deal with variations yet.

Help for the needy

When your pupil has difficulty reading a word, don't immediately jump in and read the word for him or her. Instead, provide *minimal* help. Aid the child only enough to push past a difficult part. Granted, you may sometimes have to help your learner all through a word. If so, when he or she finally manages to read the word, say something like, "But I don't think you could do that again — could you, Delphinium?" and, of course, the child will do so. A look of mock astonishment and admiration on your part will work magic in building the child's confidence.

A few seconds later, return to the troublesome word, saying, "I'll bet you've forgotten how to read it now." If you haven't left it too long since the child's last reading of the word, he or she will quickly oblige. Another show of dumbfounded amazement by you will probably draw a smile from the child, and you have the beginning of a comic caper to repeat after ever-lengthening periods of time. By such means the child will become expert in reading the word.

Sometimes, a child may begin to show aversion to reading a word because it is difficult. If so, you might go all out in your help by providing the answer to your question in the way you ask it: "I'll bet you can't read the word *Tuh-A-Puh* — **TAP**, Wolfgang."

Step 10: the

Your pupil will soon be reading sentences. But first, he or she must learn a few special words needed for the construction of sentences. Three such words are *the, that,* and *this.* Unfortunately, beginning readers have difficulty distinguishing between these three words, so we will space the learning of each to reduce confusion.

We begin with *the,* and, as you perhaps realize, teaching *the* raises a special problem because we're obliged to teach a combination of letters — *TH* — when we'd prefer to teach only single letters. Worse, we haven't even taught *H* yet. And a final problem, the sound represented by *E* in *the* isn't the sound we want your pupil to associate with this letter.

Fortunately, there is a way around these problems. We do this by using lower-case instead of upper-case letters — thus, **the**. When teaching **the**, our teachers move their fingers slowly beneath the word, giving one sound to **th**, and another sound to **e**. To sound **th** correctly, clasp the front part of your tongue loosely between your teeth, then give a long groan. This is the same sound you would make if you spoke *the* very slowly. The sound given to **e** is little more than a grunt. Again, by voicing **the** slowly you will detect the quality of grunt needed.

An incidental note: *e* in the word *the* is pronounced differently by some people depending on the word that follows it. If the next word begins with a vowel, *the* is sometimes pronounced *thee.* Check your own pronunciation of *the* by speaking the following two phrases slowly: "to the bank" and "to the attic." We want your child to assign to *e* the sound it receives in the first phrase.

Have your pupil periodically sound out the components of **the**, then say the word. If well exercised in sounding **the**, your learner is less likely to be confused when we introduce **thAT** in step 19 and **thIS** in step 28, which brings us to the matter of review.

The importance of review

There are two forms of progress in reading, as in most matters. One form of progress is achieved when a learner is able to move ahead with new, more difficult work. Another form of progress is achieved when a learner demonstrates greater skill with previously learned material. As a rule, parents and teachers prefer the first form of progress because a pupil's speedy advancement reflects well on their teaching ability. However, pupils often favor the second form because facility and speed make them look smart.

The simple, stepped manner in which material in this chapter is presented invites a constant advancement to new material. However, if, while moving ahead, your pupil is forgetting material learned earlier, then pushing ahead isn't really advancement at all. So review constantly.

Step 11: H

We now introduce properly the letter **H**, which, if you taught **the** correctly, won't be associated in your pupil's mind with the *h* in *the*. **H** is another breathed, not voiced, sound which we will show as *Huh*. This is an easy sound to produce. Just breathe out quickly, as you would onto the surface of a mirror before wiping it clean, and you will make the sound of *Huh* correctly. No voice, no grunt — just air, a sound that won't travel more than a few feet if made correctly.

Step 12: HAT

Your learner can now read the word **HAT**.

Children's names

One of the first words children ask to see in print is their name, which is regrettable for two reasons. First, you are then obliged to present a string of letters to the learner when we'd prefer to deal with just two or three at a time. Second, the letters in names often don't represent the sounds we want children to immediately associate with those letters.

For example, take the name *George*. Here, the *G* is given a different sound from the one we want the pupil to learn first (step 15). Take another: *Mary.* The *AR* letter combination is introduced when, for the moment, we want to deal only with the sound of single letters (on top of which the *AR* combination doesn't even convey its usual sound — as in *march, part,* and *start* — but conveys, instead, the sound normally represented by *ER* — as in the word *merry*).

Much might be written about the phonic pitfalls to be encountered in many common names, but we have more important matters to consider. To whatever extent you can, steer clear of names.

Step 13: O
The next sound to be learned is for **O**, sounded not as in *owe,* but as in *awe.* Just drop your jaw to its fullest and say *awe.*

Step 14: Words using O
Your learner is now able to read the words **HOT, HOP, TOP, POP, POT, COT,** and **COP**.

You may now see how the phonic system, though apparently slow to start, accelerates the learner's reading ability as each new sound symbol is mastered. Having learned only seven letter sounds, your child can now read (with practice, of course) eighteen words.

Extra words
It may have occurred to you that additional words might be composed from the sound symbols your pupil now knows. It's true. However, I have avoided some such words because of their obscurity, e.g. *tot, pub,* and *hub,* or because they employ letter combinations we don't want to introduce yet, as in the words *out, coat,* and *path* (in which *th* is sounded differently from *th* in the word *the*). Be wary therefore about introducing additional words to the program.

Step 15: G
G is next, sounded *not* as *jee.* Please forget *jee.* The sound we want associated with this sound-symbol is imperfectly presented by the letters **Guh**. The **uh** part is voiced, but it is cut off quickly. Now there's a puzzle! How quickly do you cut off the sound? The best help I can give you is to get back to the last scene in your film. Your final line, shouted

— *not* whispered — to Terence, is, "G-G-Great g-g-gadzooks, man, don't g-g-grapple with that g-g-grenade. It . . ." BOOM! (Too bad.) However, that closing line — which may live long in theatergoers' memories — gave you the opportunity to produce the abrupt **Guh** sound several times.

Step 16: Words using G

Your pupil can now begin working with **HUG**, **GOT**, **TAG**, **TUG**, **HOG**, **GAG**, and **GAP**.

The matter of rewards

Learning to read is a form of work for children, and though we will be using teaching methods that are both engaging and entertaining, your reading venture will be even more pleasurable if you add some immediate form of compensation for effort expended. Assuredly, reading will eventually provide its own bountiful reward for your child when he or she can read skilfully. Until then, however — and particularly if your pupil is a preschooler — there is justification for compensating him or her in some way to make up for the missing, yet-to-be-realized pleasures of reading.

Rewards fill this need. Though some educators denounce the practice of giving extrinsic reward for educational effort, it is nevertheless wise to employ the procedure in three situations: to prompt pupils to engage in an activity that wouldn't normally interest them; to engage pupils in an activity they have previously avoided; and to provide pupils with enough basic skill in a complex subject so they can begin enjoying the intrinsic pleasures of that subject. This last condition prevails in teaching reading.

It might be noted in passing that educators argue less about *whether* rewards should be given than *what sort* of rewards are suitable. Concern is rarely voiced when rewards take the form of smiles and praise — which may, in fact, be the only rewards needed in your teaching situation.

Compliments are ideal for all teaching situations, and the parent or teacher who parcels them out lavishly will keep the learner's spirits high and maintain his or her striving mechanism at full throttle. The following igniters of enthusiasm may help you think of others even better suited to your teaching situation:

Hey, that's terrific!	Good, good, good!
You're learning *so* quickly!	Super!
Nice going!	That's much better!
Way to go!	That's the best yet!
My, that's wonderful!	Excellent!
You're getting *so* good at this!	A big improvement!

Step 17: B

Next, we introduce the letter **B**, normally given the sound *bee*. Please forget *bee*. The sound we want your pupil to associate with this letter is, like **Guh**, a cut off sound. If you begin to say the word *book*, then quickly cut off the *ook*, you will approximate the desired sound: a sound we will represent as **Buh**. Employ our stuttering procedure — at which you are probably now expert — in speaking, *not* whispering, "B-B-Broccoli b-b-builds b-b-brains." Any one of those nine **Buh**s will fill your need admirably.

Step 18: Words using B

We can now add the words **BAG**, **BAT**, **BUG**, **TUB**, **CUB**, **CAB**, **COB**, **BOB**, and **BUT** to your pupil's reading list.

Step 19: thAT

It's time now to introduce another important word for the eventual construction of sentences: **thAT**. The **th** continues to receive the special sound described in step 10. *A* and *T* are sounded in the regular manner.

If your pupil has had plenty of exercise in reading **the**, he or she should have little difficulty in distinguishing between **the** and **thAT**.

Step 20: I

The sound *eye* is associated with the letter **I**. But we don't want the *eye* sound. If you speak the words *hit*, *hip*, and *sit*, the sound in the middle of each word is the one we want.

Step 21: Words using I

We can now add the words **PIG**, **BIT**, **HIT**, **TIP**, **HIP**, **BIB**, and **BIG** to your reading list.

An approach to reading without clues

Because your pupil can now read about forty words, the thought might occur to you that, by learning just one or two additional words, he or she could already be reading sentences. You're right. But there's a special reason why we're not rushing into the reading of sentences. It has to do with context clues.

You may remember, from step 3, that the configuration clue was one of the word-attack tricks intended to compensate for a learner's uncertain knowledge of letter sounds. Another of the tricks, called the *context clue*, advises the learner to study the entire sentence in order to puzzle out a particular word he or she can't read. So the learner who can't read the word *sits* in the sentence "The dog sits on the rug," might guess the right word by reading the other words in the sentence. "The dog [does something] on the rug." Could it be *sits*? A good guess. Of course, the child might also guess *jumps, eats, lies, sleeps,* or *plays*. However, this wouldn't bother some experts who claim that guesses of this sort are not to be regarded as errors in reading. (No, I'm not kidding — it's the truth!)

Another word-attack trick frequently advocated is called the *picture clue*. A learner using picture clues would study the accompanying illustration to see what the dog is doing on the rug. No illustration? Well, we all have those days, though it's particularly tough when you're young.

These counterfeit methods of reading would be amusing, except that so many youngsters are led to believe they are treading a tested, proven, traditional path to literacy. When children stumble and fail, they naively blame themselves, not the method.

By teaching single, unrelated words — as we are doing — rather than sentences, we oblige the learner to rely solely on the letter sounds for identifying words. If the learner stumbles, we know immediately which letters should receive more attention and practice.

Step 22: R

The sound we want for **R** isn't *ar*. The sound we want is **ur**. Part your lips, then purse them — as if you were going to kiss a hippopotamus; thrust your jaw forward and groan. R-R-Right?

Step 23: Words using R

Add **RAT**, **RUG**, **RUB**, **ROB**, **RAG**, **RIP**, and **RIB** to your reading list. Depending on the age of your pupil, you might be able to introduce words with four letters, but these can be tricky. If your learner shows stress, back off and save these words for a later session: **TRIP**, **TRAP**, **GRAB**, **CRIB**, **CRAB**, and **BRAG**.

Step 24: N

For the letter **N**, forget the sound *en*. The sound we want is just a clear and unbroken hum with the lips parted slightly, a wisp of a smile, the front of the tongue pressed against the palate, and the sound emitted from the nose.

Step 25: Words using N

Your reading list is now extended by the words **IN**, **ON**, **PIN**, **PAN**, **ANT**, **RUN**, **RAN**, **CAN**, **NOT**, **BUN**, **GUN**, **TIN**, **NUT**, **NIP**, and **NAP**.

Depending on the maturity of your learner, you might introduce the *NG* ending and proceed with **HANG**, **BANG**, **RING**, and **RUNG**. The sounds of *N* and *G* in these words are linked so quickly that you might have to spend extra time helping your pupil with the quick sound-transfer. **RUNG** is the best word to start with because most of it is the simple word *run*. Have your pupil read **RUN**, then add the **G**. Don't expect him or her to grasp the idea immediately. To the child, this is a new form of magic. With practice and a speeding up of the letter sounds — and plenty of help — your pupil will learn to skim quickly from the **N** to the **G**.

Step 26: S

The sound we want for **S** isn't *ess*, but just an unbroken hiss without voiced accompaniment: the noise theatergoers used to make when the villain appeared onstage.

Step 27: Words using S

We can now add the following words to your reading list: **SIT, SAT, BUS, SUN, GAS, PASS, RUST, STOP,** and **SPIN,** and, if your pupil can handle the *NG* ending (and word tense), **SONG, SING, SANG, STUNT, STRING,** and **STRONG.**

You might show your pupil how, by the addition of a final *S,* a word can be changed from singular to plural: **CATS, POTS, CUPS,** and so on. But be careful to avoid presenting a word in which the final *S* is buzzed rather than hissed, as occurs in the words *pins* and *pans.*

Step 28: thIS

Follow the same procedure with **thIS** that you did for **the** and **thAT,** giving the **th** that special sound described in step 10. If your pupil has been well exercised in reading **the** and **thAT,** he or she will more easily distinguish between **the, thAT,** and **thIS.** But don't worry if there is confusion. Just act as if it isn't important and get in a little extra practice.

Step 29: D

Forget the sound *dee.* The sound we want for this letter, which we will show as **Duh,** stops quickly when the tongue leaves the roof of the mouth. This will happen several times if you stutter the universal caution for swimmers, "D-D-Don't d-d-drink and d-d-dive."

Step 30: Words using D

Your pupil might now begin reading **DOG, DIG, HID, DOT, ADD, BAD, PAD, AND, HAND, SAND,** and **BAND.** Because the sequence of letters **DR** can be difficult for a learner, you might spend extra time helping him or her read **DRIP, DROP,** and **DRAG.**

Step 31: E

The sound usually associated with **E** (*ee*) isn't the sound we want. *Eh* comes closer to it: the sound we hear in the middle of the words *bed, bet,* and *beg.* This sound is just a steady unwavering tone.

Step 32: Words using E

When your pupil has learned the *eh* sound, you can introduce **RED**, **HEN**, **PEN**, **TEN**, **BED**, **BEG**, **BET**, **PET**, **NET**, and **RENT**. Perhaps, with extra coaching for the *ST* combination, he or she might be able to read **STEP**, **NEST**, **PEST**, **BEST**, and **REST**.

You and your pupil have now learned fifteen letter sounds, which we have combined in various ways to make more than a hundred words. The remaining eleven letter sounds are described in chapter 8 along with instructions for teaching the first two hundred sentences. Those eleven sounds are presented in the following order: *F, L, M, J, W, V, X, Z, QU.* The letters *Y* and *K* will be taught in an incidental way.

PART TWO

TEACHING THE FIRST 100 WORDS

Introduction to Part Two

Teachers at the Institute find that five or ten minutes of instruction each day, for five or fewer days a week, is one hundred percent effective in teaching preschoolers as young as two to read. But how many parents or teachers will want to limit their instruction to such brief and intermittent lessons? Letters received from readers of my book *Teach Your Child to Read in 60 Days* showed that most parents gave between forty-five and sixty minutes a day to their reading programs — not all in a single block of instruction, but rather in two or three reading sessions a day: perhaps in a brief morning session before going to work, a before-supper session, and a final before-bed session.

However, to provide a more comfortable schedule for parents who can't devote this much time each day to reading instruction, yet who think ten minutes is too little, let's settle on a program of thirty minutes a day. You, the teacher — meaning parent, caregiver, or schoolteacher — can divide the thirty minutes any way you wish. You can, in fact, shorten or lengthen your daily involvement without reducing the general effectiveness of the system. Naturally, the more time you devote to the program each day, the more quickly your learner or learners will advance. But more important than the *length* of time you spend teaching, is the *way* those moments are spent. And that brings us to an important factor in the learning process.

There is a telephone number at the bottom of page 60. Please turn to that page and study the number for not longer than five seconds. By doing so you will help to illustrate an important detail in the workings of the mind.

If you have looked at the number, we can proceed.

Now think of a single house standing alone in the middle of nowhere. The house is surrounded by exceedingly tall grass, about two meters high (over six feet). The growth is so thick that, as we walk slowly away from the house, our view of it soon becomes obscured by the grass. Of necessity, we must trample some of the grass to push through, however, it rises behind us slowly to its original upright position, so that, looking back, we have difficulty seeing where we have trodden. As we continue walking, we come to a clearing. No more grass. On all sides we see routine events of daily life going on.

The house is intended to represent our brain. The tall grass represents the neural circuitry that connects information stored in our brain to our conscious daily life (the clearing). Were you able to picture all this in your mind? OK, what is the number at the bottom of page 60? *That's* what we left at the house.

The purpose of this outlandish exercise with house, grass, and clearing is to provide a rough, yet workable, representation of the way our memory works. If you forgot the number on page 60, you are one of us — the multitude who have no special talent for remembering such matters. (On the other hand, if you *did* remember the number, we can only hope that those around you respectfully appreciate your unusual powers.)

If you were to look at the number again, you would be starting back at the house. Let's suppose that this time after looking at the number you moved more quickly through the grass and, on reaching the clearing, you quickly returned to the house. Because your return was speedy, the grass wouldn't have time to completely regain its upright position, and you could find your original route through it. The more trips you make to and from the house with — at first — only a short delay between trips, the more distinguishable the route becomes, which then permits you to leave longer periods between trips and still remember the information. At last, of course, information that was originally difficult to remember, even one day later, becomes easy to remember a week, a month, or even a year later.

The bottom line is this: constant, repeated recall gives us easy access to information stored in our brains. You remember your own telephone number because you have had to recall it many times — when you give the number to this or that person, and when you write it down on various forms and applications. But remembering that number probably wasn't easy when the telephone company first assigned it to you. It was the repeated need to remember that particular set of digits that eventually created a well-defined route through the grass.

Effective remembering — which we might also call *learning* — is hastened by repeated recall, and it is more quickly achieved when the recalls are, at first, only briefly separated. Repetition and review are therefore essential for rapid learning, so we will employ plenty of repetition and review in our teaching procedures. And the final accelerator of speedy learning — several short sessions each day rather than a single long session — is one I hope all teachers will employ.

Here is a brief guide to the chapters in part 2. Please note that though the content of chapter 3 might not seem to hold much value for anyone wishing to teach an older child, the procedures described in that chapter can help you begin thinking in new ways about teaching. Chapter 3 therefore provides a good base from which to launch your own program. In a similar vein, each of the other chapters, though apparently written for reaching goals different from the one you are most interested in, contains information which, to avoid repetition, could not be included in every chapter. Such information will serve you well as you proceed with your own program.

Chapter 3, *Teaching a Preschooler,* describes how to teach the basic information contained in chapter 2 in a way that ensures rapid reading progress.

Chapter 4, *Babysitters and Caregivers as Teachers,* shows how to become the most popular babysitter on the block — or possibly in the entire neighborhood — while making a major contribution to children's lives and securing, as a bonus, valuable teaching experience that will eventually make impressive reading on a job résumé.

Chapter 5, *Teaching in a Daycare Center or Nursery School,* will let you add intellectual stimulation to the predominantly arts/crafts/socialization programs common in daycare centers (and to a lesser extent, in nursery schools). The text emphasizes the benefits that staff can gain in pride of accomplishment, and that management can gain in prestige and increased revenue.

Chapter 6, *Kindergarten and Grade 1 Teachers,* gives kindergarten teachers a chance to play a greater role in children's academic advancement, and shows grade 1 teachers how to graduate a completely literate class of children in ten months.

Chapter 7, *Teaching Your Schoolchild,* tells how to speed a schoolchild's reading advancement or remedy his or her faulty reading, and how (or whether) to form a working partnership with the child's schoolteacher.

The number is 374-9258.

3

Teaching a
Preschooler

Read this chapter completely before beginning your reading program. Some matters dealt with in this chapter could influence the way you prepare for the program. Here we put to use the basic information given in chapter 2 in a way that assures the easy and rapid progress of a preschool-age child.

A preschooler, technically speaking (and even legally speaking), is a child who hasn't yet reached age six. In fact, because of the usual cut-off age-date for entry into grade 1, a child can be almost seven before the law requires his or her presence in school. (Some parents don't realize that kindergarten isn't obligatory.) In any case, though two-year-olds and five-year-olds are technically preschoolers, a great difference normally exists in how they learn. Older children usually have more advanced thinking ability, better concentration, and a longer attention span. But, and but again, this isn't justification for delaying a two-year-old's instruction simply because he or she will eventually be easier to teach. The earlier a child starts reading, the greater potential benefit to the child.

To accommodate the wide differences in preschool learning ability, we will aim our instruction at a child of middle preschool age. Let's begin by fleshing out a hypothetical preschooler to be our pupil — a three-and-a-half-year-old. We'll call her Marcia. By creating a fictitious pupil, and by considering problems that might arise in teaching her (by a fictitious parent we will create), we can deal with the various problems you too might face when teaching your child, and we will be able to do so without constant use of the expressions *your child*, *he or she*, and *him or her*. If your child is younger than Marcia, you can lengthen each step of the proceedings and slow your rate of progress. If your preschooler is older, you can shorten each step and quicken your progress.

It doesn't matter whether Marcia is anxious to begin reading, nor even that she knows what reading is, nor, lastly, that she ever sees anyone reading in the home. From Marcia's point of view, all she'll be doing is playing a game.

SETTING THE STAGE

Use of the word *stage* is appropriate. Experience shows that when teaching reading (or when teaching *any* subject, for that matter) children's rapt attention and ready cooperation are more quickly won if showmanship, razzle-dazzle, and a few laughs are thrown in — matters of great importance to us during the relatively slow-moving first steps of reading advancement. But later, when children see how the letter code works and see how squiggles on paper can blossom into wonders of meaning — ah! then the game changes, and the inherent fascination of reading begins to work in our favor. In the beginning, though, we will resort to whatever showbiz techniques and strategies prove effective for capturing Marcia's attention and speeding her merrily along the path to literacy.

Each child is different. And parent–child relationships vary. Home environments, too, can differ greatly. The procedures presented here — some of them carnival-like — and the motivational strategies employed may be wholly unnecessary — even inappropriate — in some homes. In other homes, though, the techniques may help parents overcome their natural reserve and encourage them to become daringly entertaining in their teaching methods. Don't feel you have to copy the procedures. Their main importance lies in prompting you to think in new ways about your own home program. So shop among the methods. Learn from them, adopt or adapt them as you choose, and settle on a system that you and your child feel comfortable with.

We begin by building a "teaching machine" — the blocks game. It's easy.

Materials for the blocks game
You will need

- a large piece of cardboard approximately 20 by 70 centimeters (about 8 by 27 inches), perhaps cut from a corrugated cardboard carton;
- strong glue or casein cement;
- an empty egg carton;
- a number of business card blanks (the backs of old cards will do);
- adhesive putty (obtainable at office supply outlets, and used for attaching notes, drawings and other paper items to walls); and
- two felt markers: one that will produce a line about two millimeters (one-sixteenth inch) wide, and a thicker marker that will produce marks about fifteen millimeters (one-half inch) wide. Daubers sold for bingo games make excellent thick markers because they give a regular width of line no matter in which direction they are moved.

Finally, you will need three blocks, perhaps made of wood. If your child has building blocks, there might be suitably-sized blocks among them. Otherwise, you could construct three small corrugated cardboard boxes to serve as blocks: about 4 by 9 by 2 centimeters (1 1/2 by 3 1/2 by 3/4 inches).

Preparing the blocks game
Your 20-by-70 centimeter piece of cardboard is the base of the teaching machine. Remove the lid from the egg carton and cut lengthwise

between the twelve cups to make two rows of six cups. Glue the two six-cup sections along one side of the corrugated cardboard base and rule lines on the base between the cups, adding three more spaces at the end as shown in figure 2. There you have it — a low-tech piece of laboratory equipment that will out-perform any computer program in speeding your child (and Marcia) entertainingly along the path to literacy.

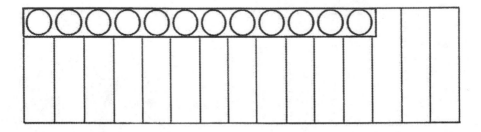

Figure 2: The blocks game

THE PLAY

When you are working with a young child, the proceedings are best conducted on the floor so the learner will have an undistorted view of the letters. Sitting at a table could give him or her a slanted or oblique-angle view of printed materials. If for some reason you must conduct your program sitting at a table, you can play the game in a different way, as described later.

Next, the stage dressing and the props. You might bring out the bath mat, for example, or some other outrageously misplaced floor covering so as to create a setting that virtually shouts, "Something new and special going on here!" A few stuffed toys propped up — perhaps in a colorful plastic basin — will fill the roles of additional pupils: a student body we will use to advantage. You might even suspend a balloon or two, or Christmas decorations, or pin a colorful calendar or some other attention-getting device to the wall. Anything goes.

If Marcia knows what *school* means, we'll say we're going to play school. And because Marcia has likely never seen a school classroom, she won't be able to adversely compare our outrageous school area to the real thing. If, on the other hand, she doesn't know what *school* means, we'll just say we're going to play a game.

Single parents will probably have less time to give to the reading program than those in two-parent homes. So, to suit our program to the most trying situations, let's assume the teaching parent is single. Though the parent could as easily be the father, we'll say it's the mother, and her name is Cynthia. Cynthia works full time while Marcia spends her days at a daycare center. And to create an even tougher teaching situation, let's assume that Marcia is a strong-willed young lady who constantly tests the limits of her mother's authority, and has achieved considerable skill in exercising the power of veto.

Cynthia, who has never taught children before, sees possible difficulty in teaching her often uncooperative daughter. She concludes that the success or failure of their reading program will depend largely on Marcia's inclination and mood, which are often unpredictable. But, being resourceful and imaginative, Cynthia has already figured out ways to win Marcia's cooperation and speed her along to literacy.

Cynthia has decided she can fit thirty minutes of instruction each day into her busy schedule: five minutes after breakfast, ten minutes before supper, and fifteen minutes before Marcia's bedtime. On the two nights Cynthia attends community college, her babysitter, Kim, will take care of the bedtime teaching session.

Cynthia has mastered the sounds of **U** and **P**, as described in chapter 2, has constructed the blocks game, and has cut three blocks with a bread knife from a thick piece of Styrofoam. Now, with markers and typing paper at hand, she is ready to begin the program.

Cynthia spreads an old bed sheet on the floor, its edges forming the boundary of the school, and attaches to the wall a class photo taken when she was in grade 4, the Dutch flag, her high-school diploma, and a travel poster: "VISIT ENGLAND." Finally, suspending a set of cowbells from the ceiling, she scatters a few cushions around to add color, and props up additional pupils in the forms of a large doll, a small doll, a stuffed rabbit, a monkey, and a teddy bear.

Ta-dah-h-h! Though the outlandish classroom setting may prompt visitors to smile, their response might in turn prompt Marcia to demonstrate her rapidly advancing reading ability.

Day 1: Scene I

Cynthia sits on the floor with Marcia in the school area, ready to begin step 1, introducing the letter **U**. The blocks game is hidden away; its eventual introduction in a couple of days will be a big event. Cynthia has explained that because teddy bear is getting to be a big boy, he'll soon be starting school. It's time he learned to read, and Marcia might like to help teach him.

With a wide marker, Cynthia prints the letter **U** about ten centimeters (four inches) high on a piece of typing paper and places it on the floor so the top and bottom are correctly positioned for Marcia.

"We want teddy bear to learn to say *uh* when he sees this shape, Marcia. Are you watching, teddy bear? Listen, now — *uh*!" She presses the teddy bear's nose into her ear. "No, that's not it. Listen to Marcia, teddy bear. She'll teach you. Go ahead, Marcia, he's listening." With a small amount of help, Marcia is soon making the correct sound.

Thrusting the bear's nose in her ear again, Cynthia announces he still can't make the sound. She taps the bear gently on the head to get his thinking mechanism functioning, and says to Marcia, "Tell you what, Marcia, maybe if you move your finger around the shape while you're making the sound, he'll get the idea." Marcia does so. Alas, teddy bear still doesn't get the message, and the expression of dismay on Cynthia's face makes Marcia smile.

On Cynthia's suggestion, Marcia makes the appropriate sound not just once, but several times, while moving her finger around the shape. Teddy bear can't miss it now — or can he? Pushing the bear's nose into her ear, Cynthia reports that he said "Urk," which draws a giggle from Marcia. However, after Marcia has performed the tracing ritual twice more, Cynthia announces with delight that the bear has actually made the sound correctly. She praises Marcia for her good teaching. But now it's time to head for the daycare center. Marcia doesn't want to stop, but she is promised more sessions later in the day.

Intermission

What did we learn? Cynthia's suggestion that Marcia move a finger around the **U** while repeating the sound several times was excellent. The intricate muscle movement required to accomplish this helped to fix the letter shape more firmly in Marcia's mind. And, while making the finger movements, Marcia uttered the appropriate sound more than twenty times.

Cynthia prints two more **U**s. She affixes one to the apartment door and props teddy bear up facing it, "so he can be learning while we're away," and is delighted to see Marcia tracing a finger around the shape for teddy bear's benefit while Cynthia searches for her keys. She takes the second **U** with her to the car and clips it to the sun visor with a clothes peg so Marcia, in the back seat, will see it.

While driving to the daycare center, Cynthia introduces Marcia to a game she calls, "What am I going to say?" After asking Marcia this question, Cynthia then makes the sound *uh*. When Marcia can't guess, Cynthia says, "Up." She tries again. This time Marcia says, "Up." Complimenting her profusely, Cynthia lets Marcia take a turn. Marcia says, "What am I going to say? *Uh.*" To add humor to the game, Cynthia responds wrongly with, "usteronkey?" No? Then, "ulpatorium?" No? How about, "uncle?" Of course, Marcia had *up* in mind all the time, but now she has been alerted to the fact that *uncle* does, in fact, start with the *uh* sound.

Continuing in this manner, and alternating between nonsense words — *ugglegooper, uptopottamus, underopatory* — and actual words — *us, umbrella,* and *Uxbridge* (where a friend lives) — Cynthia gradually sensitizes Marcia's hearing to beginning sounds of words. Naturally, Cynthia uses nonsense words only when responding to Marcia's query, and uses correct words when asking Marcia to guess.

Cynthia learned something too. Having stopped the reading lesson while Marcia wanted to continue, Cynthia created a store of enthusiasm in Marcia. As a result, the continuation of teddy bear's education was Marcia's first concern when Cynthia picked her up at the daycare that afternoon. Seeing how cutting off or denying an activity heightened Marcia's interest, Cynthia made a note to employ this strategy to its fullest extent in the future.

Scene II

Arriving home, Cynthia immediately sets Marcia to work for teddy bear's advancement. She props the bear up nearby, gives Marcia the front page of a newspaper, and asks her to circle with a crayon all the **U**s she can find in the headlines. While Marcia is doing this, Cynthia prepares supper.

With pots bubbling on the stove, Cynthia examines Marcia's efforts, congratulates her, and shows teddy bear the result. He can't fail to identify the letter now! Time for their ten-minute reading session.

Alas, as you might guess, the bear finds the sounding of **U** no easier than identifying craters on the moon, and he whispers a succession of absurdities into Cynthia's ear — to Marcia's delight. Recalling from her babysitting days the great amusement children find in the misadventures of the world's worst maid, Amelia Bedelia (described in several books), Cynthia decides to bring another blundering pupil into the drama. She says the following, speaking the italicized words in a high-pitched voice, "*I can do that. It's easy.* Who said that? *Me, Mr. Monkey.*" Cynthia removes the monkey from the plastic basin.

Of course Marcia knows the monkey's voice is really Cynthia's, but Cynthia knows that children tend to believe what they want to believe. As long as humor is involved, and Marcia comes off looking clever, she will go along with the ventriloquist caper.

"Well, if you're so smart, Mr. Monkey, perhaps you'd like to make the sound for this shape here. *It's too easy. Any dummy can do that.* Then go ahead, do it." Cynthia manipulates the monkey so it looks up, down, and in all directions, humming and stalling for time. Marcia begins to smile.

"We're waiting, Mr. Monkey. Let's hear you say **uh**. *It's too easy. Besides, I'm not in the mood.* You mean you can't do it. *I can, I can. It's m-m-m. It's . . . it's oo-o-ogle.*" Marcia glows with a feeling of superiority. Cynthia puts the monkey back in the basin, saying no one likes a show-off — especially one who can't do what he says he can, and he'd better pay attention or he'll never get into *any* school.

The session ends and supper is served. Later, while Marcia is splashing in the nearby bathtub, Cynthia puts the dishes into the "someday" basin under the sink and makes notes on their reading progress.

Scene III

Still later, Marcia, now in her nightgown, is busy getting teddy bear ready for bed. Time for the final fifteen-minute reading session. Anticipating (by means of the sixth sense parents develop) possible reluctance by Marcia to engage in another reading session so soon after the last one, Cynthia waits until Marcia is watching her, then glances at her watch. "I don't think we can give teddy bear another lesson tonight, we haven't time."

That does it! Here is Marcia's opportunity to exercise a veto *and* delay going to bed too — a double play! She implores Cynthia to let her teach the bear. With seeming reluctance, Cynthia agrees, and by glancing apprehensively at her watch throughout the session keeps Marcia's interest at high pitch. Cynthia makes a series of **U**s on typing paper, and Marcia sounds each as it is printed. After filling a page with these, they find and circle **U**s in newspaper headlines. Fifteen minutes are up and it's time for bed.

Cynthia prints a larger **U**, twenty centimeters (about eight inches) high, on a piece of typing paper and, standing on the kitchen steps, affixes it to the ceiling over Marcia's bed. Now the bear — who will be lying beside Marcia — will be able to view the shape for a couple of minutes before lights out.

Cynthia was tempted to move on to step 2 — the letter **P** — today, but knowing that a slow, simple beginning will ensure eventual quick progress, she refrained from doing so. Prompted by a final thought, Cynthia prints two more **U**s, affixing one to the bathroom wall at an appropriate height and the other to the refrigerator door.

Day 2: Introducing the blocks game

To begin the morning session, Cynthia reviews the letter **U** briefly before introducing **P**. She follows the same procedures that she used with **U**, printing a **P** about ten centimeters high and inviting Marcia to trace the shape with her finger while repeating the appropriate *Puh* sound for the bear and the monkey.

Later in the day, Cynthia begins the before-supper session by reviewing **U** briefly, then continues with **P**. Marcia traces her finger around **P**, voicing *Puh* repeatedly for the bear and monkey who, though now able to sound both letters, always manage to attach the wrong sound to each. The braggart monkey's excuse, of course, is that he is merely testing Marcia and the bear.

Caught up now in the educational drama presented by the dunce bear and monkey, Marcia works hard to improve their performance. Though the bear and the monkey are frustrating pupils, they try to make amends by praising Marcia's teaching ability. The bear whispers into Cynthia's ear, whereupon she divulges, "Teddy bear thinks you're a wonderful teacher, and he says he's going to try a lot harder." The monkey brazenly states, "*You know, Marcia, I'm the greatest, but I'm beginning to think you're almost as smart as I am.*"

As the session ends, Marcia's interest and curiosity are piqued when Cynthia hints they might play the blocks game later. What, indeed, is the blocks game? You'll see.

Supper finished, and bath-time in full swing, little urging is needed to get Marcia out of the tub to discover the wonders of the blocks game.

Setting up the blocks game

Here are some instructions Cynthia — and other parents — will need to follow in preparation for the blocks game.

Print a large **U** on a business card blank (or on the back of an old business card), and a **P** on another business card. If necessary, trim the cards to fit the size of your blocks, and affix them to two blocks with small blobs of adhesive putty.

If for some reason you are playing the game at a table, not on the floor, you can ensure your child a good view of the printed matter by standing the cards up — done by cutting two slits in the bottom edge (figure 3) — instead of affixing them to blocks.

Figure 3: An alternative to using blocks

Position the blocks as shown in figure 4. It doesn't matter in which order the blocks are initially placed, because they will be changing position throughout the game. Place a small reward in each of the twelve cups of the egg box.

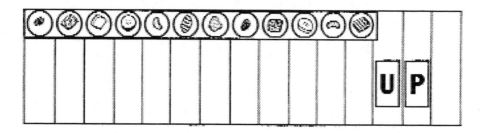

Figure 4: The blocks game, powered with rewards

A word about rewards. Medals are favored by military people. Money is popular with employees. But small children are stomach oriented, and one is wise to pay in whatever currency is valued most. The reward that goes into each cup could be a small amount of food: a raisin, half a shelled peanut, a morsel of breakfast food (even a single corn flake) or snack food, a postage-stamp-sized piece of toast, a thin slice of carrot, or a tiny piece of apple, pear, pineapple, or almost any other fruit. Varying the reward from cup to cup will provide maximum appeal.

Keep edible rewards small so they won't upset the child's appetite for regular meals. And it goes without saying that reward foodstuffs should not include any that are essential for the child's balanced daily diet; edible rewards should always be items the child could easily do without.

As an alternative to food, rewards might be stickers, or tokens that eventually secure some larger reward, or beads which, when collected in quantity, permit the child to string a necklace (in itself an excellent exercise for advancing hand-eye coordination). Of course, for a child younger than three, caution must be observed about using small hard reward items that could pose a choking hazard.

Playing the game

Cynthia moves the first, or end, block over the other block and places it beside the first cup (figure 5). After sounding the **P** and **U** correctly,

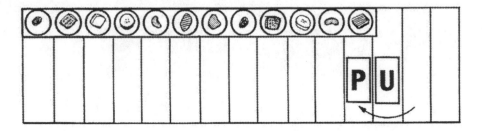

Figure 5: The parent's first move

she removes the reward from the first cup and pops it into her mouth. Seeing the interesting way food morsels can be made to travel from the egg cups to her stomach, Marcia moves what is now the end block — with slight help from Cynthia — over the other block, places it beside the second cup, sounds the **U** and **P**, and takes the reward in the second cup (figure 6). *What a tasty game,* Marcia thinks, as she and Cynthia continue munchingly down the board. In all, Marcia will sound each of the two letters a total of six times, and hear Cynthia sound them six times. Soon the game will promote many more repetitions.

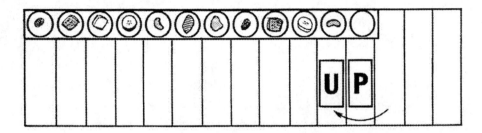

Figure 6: The child's first move

Cynthia already sees great value in playing up the bear's struggle — and inability — to collect a reward: a sad plight easily worsened by having the monkey ridicule the bear's performance. As Marcia's sympathy and protective instinct for the bear are aroused, the youngster becomes emotionally caught up in the proceedings and will want to play the game all the more (the same hook that keeps soap operas running).

Why the theatrics?

Some parents may wonder why so much attention is given to theatrical effect and motivation when they themselves see little need for such practices. The antics are intended to help guarantee success even in homes where circumstances may not favor a child's learning to read. Again, each parent should create a way of teaching that is best suited to the specific child and parent.

Needless to say, Marcia finds the blocks game fascinating and, even after three games, wants to continue. But Cynthia ends the session, and Marcia takes consolation in eating her rewards. (On Cynthia's suggestion, Marcia stockpiled the edibles for a great banquet at the end of the session, an arrangement that spares Cynthia from having to wait for Marcia to finish chewing after each turn.)

Day 3: First words

Cynthia is now ready to proceed to step 3: the first words. After breakfast, she shows Marcia two large cards bearing **UP** and **PUP**. Cynthia begins by sounding the **U** and the **P** in **UP** from left to right, and repeats the procedure, gradually increasing the speed until she is saying, "up." Cynthia points to the ceiling in the hope that Marcia may see the connection between letters, letter sounds, and the direction indicated. She continues to repeat, "up," now gradually reducing the speed of her sounds until she is once again voicing two distinct letter sounds. We call this procedure the *blending ritual.*

Cynthia then repeats the same ritual with **PUP**, and makes a rough drawing of a puppy. From Marcia's uncertain response to both **UP** and **PUP**, Cynthia sees that the ritual may have to be repeated a few times before squiggles-on-cards, quickened sounds, and something-in-the-visible-world are compressed into a unique thought in Marcia's mind.

In preparation for tomorrow's program, Cynthia prints **UP** on five cards, and **PUP** on five more — one each for the blocks game, and for teddy bear to study on the apartment door, for the sun visor in the car, for the bathroom, and for the refrigerator.

There is no knowing when Marcia — or any child — is going to grasp the idea that the sounds of individual letters can compress into the sound sequence (or sound sandwich?) that creates a word. One child may get the idea in a week; another may take a month or more. However, grasping this notion *isn't* important at the moment. By continuing the blending ritual periodically, a parent can lead a child to gradually understand a procedure that seems to us simplicity itself.

Planning to introduce **C** later in the day, Cynthia plays "What am I going to say?" (described on page 67) with the *Cuh* sound while driving Marcia to the daycare center. The words *candy, custard, cuddle,* and *cat* crop up in the game, and, most importantly, *cup,* the next word Marcia will learn.

The before-supper session starts with a review of **UP** and **PUP**. Then, in preparation for step 4, Cynthia prints **C** ten centimeters high for Marcia to trace around with her finger, then another **C** twenty-centimeters high for the ceiling above Marcia's bed, and finally, five more **C**s on business cards; one each for the blocks game, the apartment door, the sun visor, the bathroom wall, and the refrigerator.

Next, Cynthia coaches Marcia in sounding *Cuh* correctly and, after affixing **C** to a block and loading up the reward cups, engages Marcia in the game, one block bearing **C**, another, **UP**, and a third, **PUP**.

Cynthia attends college tonight so, when Kim, the babysitter, arrives, Cynthia spends a few moments explaining the sounds of the letters and the procedures for Kim to follow with Marcia — the business of finding and circling **U**s, **P**s, and **C**s in newspaper headlines, and the blocks game.

Day 4: Going solo

At the after-breakfast session, Marcia shows surprising ease in sounding the letters (which makes Cynthia wonder what time Marcia got to bed last night under Kim's guidance). Cynthia goes through the blending ritual with **UP**, "*uh Puh* — up," and **PUP**, "*Puh uh Puh* — pup," then coaches Marcia in doing the same for teddy bear's benefit. He responds, "*Uh Puh* — window," and, "*Uh Puh* — banana." Cynthia goes through the blending ritual with **CUP** (*Cuh uh Puh*) (step 5), then coaches Marcia in doing the same for Mr. Monkey, who manages, "*Cuh uh Puh* — kangaroo," then, "*Cuh uh Puh* — cookie," to Marcia's delight.

Three blocks are used in the before-supper game with **UP** on one, **PUP** on a second, and **CUP** on the third block. Now, for teddy bear's advancement, Marcia must sound the individual letters, then speak the word (regardless of whether she understands the connection between the letter sounds and the word itself, an understanding that will eventually click into place all on its own).

Cynthia plays one game of blocks with Marcia. Then, she points out that, since Marcia is teddy bear's teacher, she should play the game by herself (and, of course, collect all the rewards instead of just half of them).

In playing the game with Cynthia, Marcia sounded forty-eight letters and pronounced each word six times. But now, playing the game alone, Marcia sounds the letters ninety-six times and pronounces each word twelve times. Marcia develops such skill in letter sounding and word pronouncing that, on one occasion, she reads the word without first sounding out the letters. Cynthia wisely calls a halt and obliges Marcia to go back and sound out the letters (see the note on page 42 concerning letter sounding).

At this point, Marcia is becoming fascinated with the technicalities of reading, so the bear and monkey begin to play a less significant role in the proceedings. But they are always ready to jump back into the ring and create comic chaos if Marcia's interest ever seems to flag.

During the final session of the day, prompted by teddy bear's desperate need for help and Mr. Monkey's annoying personification of "Mr. Know-all," Marcia is induced to play *three* games of blocks on her own, which requires the sounding of letters 288 times and the pronouncing of the three words 36 times each. The ability of the blocks game to induce a great many recalls, with a consequent acceleration of learning, will now be apparent.

And so on . . . .

Having become an enjoyable daily ritual for both Cynthia and Marcia, their program continues steadily and uninterruptedly. However, our fictitious Marcia's reading advancement as a day-to-day adventure may cause a problem for readers of this book. Children whose advancement is slower than Marcia's might be regarded as performing poorly. The truth is that children learn to read at greatly varying speeds. Marcia's progress had to be shown as steady and sure because if we were to include the various disruptions that can slow a child's advancement — car trouble, illness, and other unforeseen difficulties — the result would be dull reading.

In any case, Cynthia and Marcia have now served their purpose. The importance of their performance lay in letting you experience vicariously a different way of teaching from what you might otherwise have pursued. The hope is that some of the procedures might be adaptable to your situation, or prompt you to think of equally effective ideas and methods.

Figures 7 to 12 show the contents of the three blocks for proceeding with steps 6 to 11 in chapter 2. As you see, the cards eventually contain more than one word.

For step 10, you can either remove from the game the card bearing **UP**, **PUP**, and **CUP**, or leave it in and introduce a fourth block to the game for the word **the**. Cards that are removed from the game should be reintroduced periodically for review. Another option is to increase the number of blocks used in the game. Up to six blocks can be used, with four words on each block, so twenty-four words are read each turn.

As each new letter and word is introduced, continue the series of activities that has now been described, never forgetting to review old material often. The activities are listed below for your reference:

1. Play "What am I going to say," to attune your child's ear to each new letter sound, then announce words that begin with the voiced sound.
2. Print each new letter ten centimeters high and encourage your child to trace around the shape with a finger while making the appropriate sound.

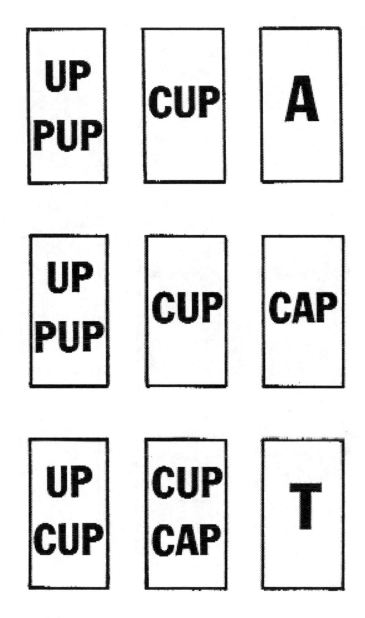

Figure 7 (top row); figure 8 (middle row); figure 9 (bottom row).

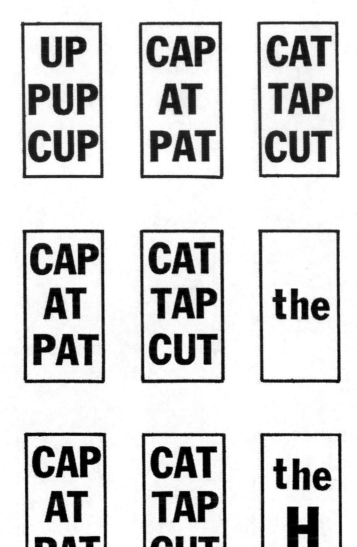

Figure 10 (top row); figure 11 (middle row); figure 12 (bottom row).

3. Play the blocks game, incorporating the new letter.

4. Display the new letter in various locations around your home.

5. Encourage your child to circle each new letter in newspaper head-lines and in advertising materials.

6. Perform the blending ritual (described on page 73) with each new word that is formed.

Take a moment to scan chapters 4, 5, and 7 for teaching ideas and games that, in their present form or with slight alteration, could add enjoyment to your program.

When you have completed step 32 in chapter 2, your child will have learned to read one hundred words or more. You will then be ready to move ahead with the first two hundred sentences, as described in chapter 8.

4

Babysitters and Caregivers as Teachers

Chapter 3 tells parents how to teach a preschooler, and chapter 5 tells parents how to teach a school-age child. But what if parents lack the time or the confidence to pursue these programs? This chapter deals with that situation, and does so in two ways: first, by introducing parents to a proven method for securing excellent, low-cost teachers to supervise their child's reading instruction — either partly or wholly; and second, by showing teenage and adult caregivers how to become excellent teachers, and when they have done so, how to find parents who will welcome the special service they are now willing and able to supply.

READING TEACHERS ON YOUR BLOCK

Teenagers will often jump at the chance to fill the role of teacher — a vocational goal they may already be thinking of — and they will welcome the chance to be trained for the role and, best of all, to be *paid for it.* For parents, employing a teenage tutor provides several advantages, a principal one being that when children are taught by an outsider they often show greater enthusiasm for learning and cooperate more readily. So, even if you, the parent, have ample time to conduct your reading program, you may still wish to capitalize occasionally on the magical influence of a good tutor.

Tending young children is a field dominated by girls, so we will assume in this text that your tutor will most likely be a girl.

How do you find tutors?

Babysitters are a good bet. Perhaps you already employ a babysitter who could handle the teaching task. If not, ask around the neighborhood, pin a note on the bulletin board at the supermarket, or, if you live in an apartment, leave a note in the laundry room.

A better idea, though, is to secure girls who are recommended. Students who perform well in school are potentially good tutors. You might therefore phone the nearest high school, describe your needs to a teacher in the upper grades, and ask him or her to have one or two capable girls call you. The leader of the local Girl Guide troop, or the secretary of a neighborhood church, may be able to recommend responsible girls. Finding one or two good tutors can lead you to others, because their best friends will likely possess the same qualities you are looking for. Your tutor might teach while you are out or at home, the latter situation leaving you free to deal with other household duties (of particular appeal to single parents). A good tutor should have a warm, charming way with children, and should teach, by her manner, considerably more than just reading. John Locke's thought-provoking description of the ideal tutor in 1693 is no less valid today:

> *Seek out somebody that may know how discreetly to frame his manners: place him in hands where you may, as much as possible, secure his innocence, cherish and nurse up the good, and gently correct and weed out any bad inclination, and settle in him good habits. This is the main point, and this being provided for, learning may be had into the bargain.* *

---

* John Locke, *Some Thoughts Concerning Education* (New York, 1964).

Girls are normally available for tutoring after school and on week-ends, except, of course, during school holidays, when they could be available any time of day. Depending on your own schedule, tutors might visit immediately after school or after supper, and perhaps on Saturday and Sunday. To secure tutoring service every day, you may need to engage several girls; tutoring more than twice a week can diminish the tutor's enthusiasm for teaching. Equally important, by employing several tutors you will have backups to call when one or the other is ill or busy with school work. One enterprising single parent employed six girls to handle a seven-day-a-week tutoring schedule.

With supervision, girls as young as nine have served admirably as tutors. However, the age of your child will have some bearing on how old the tutor should be. If your child is seven or eight, a nine-year-old tutor will have less influence and control than a sixteen-year-old.

How would the arrangement work?

By referring to the appropriate chapters in this book, you could plan each reading session for the tutor and have her follow your detailed instructions. Or you might teach briefly at the beginning of each session to make sure the tutor understands what is to be taught and how to teach it, then turn the task over to her, periodically monitoring her adherence to the procedures you have prescribed. Or you might simply issue loose guidelines within which the tutor would operate, and let her puzzle out the details. Or, finally, if the tutor is mature and bright, you might just give her this book and let her pursue the program unassisted.

How much should you pay tutors?

Payment would depend on the age of the tutor and perhaps on the distance she must travel to your home. If a girl is old enough to babysit, she is accustomed to receiving a standard rate for doing little more than watching TV, completing homework, or reading, so she might justifiably expect more than the regular babysitting fee. Fifteen- and sixteen-year-olds might be paid as much as twice the regular babysitting rate. But nine-, ten-, and eleven-year-olds who, because of their youth may not get a chance to earn money babysitting, will probably be delighted to receive just the regular babysitting rate — or even less. Thus, by finding younger tutors — some of whom have a genius for charming and winning the cooperation of young children — you can secure excellent tutoring at a low cost.

Now let's consider the situation from the viewpoint of those who will be tutoring.

BABYSITTERS AS READING TEACHERS

There aren't many career opportunities open for nine-year-olds. One you might consider, though — if, in fact, you *are* nine (and subject, of course, to your parents' approval) — is teaching. But you're probably older than nine. I mention that age only because, of the many youngsters who taught my own children, the youngest were nine. And they did a wonderful job.

Here was the situation. As a single parent raising a two-year-old and a three-year-old, I was usually too tired on arriving home from work to handle the household chores as well as the early education I wanted my daughters to have. By hiring several youngsters, ages nine to sixteen, I was able to prepare supper and deal with other routine tasks while the tutors worked their teaching magic.

I mention the matter only to build your self-confidence. It seems to me that if nine-year-olds can teach, so can you — whatever your age or lack of experience. Naturally, I had to tell the youngsters what to teach and how to teach it. But I plan to do the same for you in this chapter. By getting the same guidance, you will be able to deliver the same good service to children in your neighborhood.

The teenage tutor

You, the reader, may not be a teenager, but an adult — perhaps a homemaker who looks after someone else's children while the parents work. Though this chapter is aimed at teenagers, the guidance given will serve adult caregivers equally well, and will let both groups make an important contribution to the intellectual and academic advancement of children in their care.

Why should babysitters bother to teach? The first and immediate benefit is that when parents learn you can teach preschoolers to read (and when, eventually, you can help schoolchildren with their reading problems, dealt with in chapter 7), your babysitting services will be prized and eagerly sought.

In teaching the first child, you will gain skill. And in gaining skill, you will gain confidence. And with skill and confidence, it may be *this home* today, *the neighborhood* tomorrow. Word will spread about the babysitter who not only minds children but teaches them to read. And to help word spread more quickly you might tack a notice on the board at the supermarket or on lampposts and at bus stops, or even distribute a brief notice to homes you know have a preschooler:

RESPONSIBLE BABYSITTER
WILL TEACH YOUR CHILD
TO READ WHILE BABYSITTING.
BEST REFERENCES. PHONE . . .

You might win the same special attention enjoyed by Mrs. P., a nursery school owner whose fame, and business, increased dramatically when it became known she was teaching preschoolers to read (see chapter 5). But wait. If, by teaching preschoolers to read, a professional early childhood education specialist created a hot news item — attracting newspaper coverage and appearances on two national TV shows — think how much hotter the news item would be if you, a teenager, accomplished the same! And if a newspaper, or a radio or TV station reported your rare service, your phone might never stop ringing. You would then be able to pick and choose your clients and charge higher fees.

A second benefit to you is that being able to teach reading means you won't be dependent solely on babysitting for money. Some parents may want you to teach their children as soon as you get home from school each day. In this case you would be justified in charging more than the babysitting fee. How much more? That would depend on your age and your expertise. The section "How much should you pay tutors?" earlier in this chapter provides a guideline.

If you have a recreation room in your home, you might hold a Saturday morning "school" and give either individual or group instruction. The latter is described in chapters 5 and 6.

Teaching a child or children to read will oblige you to think ahead and decide what you are going to teach, how and when to move on, and what materials you need to collect or construct. In short, the teaching adventure will provide a valuable exercise in decision-making, planning, and organization — qualities treasured by all employers, that will stand you in good stead when you eventually enter the adult job market.

Looking to the future, perhaps you have thought of becoming a schoolteacher, a social worker, or a nursery school or daycare teacher. The teaching experience you gain now will look good on any résumé you submit to a teachers' college, a training institute, or any eventual prospective employer in the child-care or education field.

Did we overlook something? Yes, indeed! Someday you may be a parent yourself. And good parenting is largely a matter of good teaching. So the expertise you gain in teaching other people's children will increase the benefits you can give your own child or children. You will learn the value of patience, yes, but you will also discover the surprising ways in which children learn. You will see what accelerates learning or slows it — all of which will be of immense value should you eventually study psychology, sociology, or any other subject dealing with human performance.

The preteen tutor

Let's suppose you are only nine, ten, eleven, or twelve. In this case, your parents may have to help you learn the steps described in chapters 2 and 3. But you don't have to learn the entire content of those chapters all at once. You need to be only one step ahead of your pupil. When you have mastered the first step or two, offer your services free to someone with a preschooler. You wouldn't be babysitting — you would be teaching while the parent is at home looking after other matters. By teaching one child, you will gain skill, and with skill, you will gain confidence. You might gain an income too, because the surprised and delighted parents might soon offer to pay you for your teaching.

Single parents are a good bet for the reasons described earlier in this chapter. They are usually happy just to have the children out of their way for a few minutes.

Work as a team!

Whether you are nine or nineteen, a good way to build confidence is to work with a friend, discussing the challenges to be met and the various ways to deal with them. Go through chapters 2 and 3 with your partner and make sure you can both make the letter sounds correctly. Then, when each of you feels comfortable with the procedures — which really aren't difficult — you will be ready to make your introductory proposal to a parent.

In fact, why don't you *both* teach the first child — as a team! Granted, you will have to divide the babysitting fee, but you will both learn from each success or minor teaching slip-up, and you will be able to assess together what produces the quickest progress.

The university-age tutor

In time, you may attend university (if, in fact, you're not already there) and you will need a larger income. Your teaching expertise will now be even more valuable. Having taught two, three, or more children, you will have the knowledge and confidence (plus the mature manner and appearance) needed to secure higher-paying teaching situations. These could include in-home tutoring for families other than those you personally know — families who may live in distant neighborhoods.

Is this a promising source of business? Emphatically, yes. Consider that parents who want tutoring for their children must normally drive to a tutoring center, and then wait around for an hour while their children receive instruction — which is usually given along with two other children. With the time spent traveling and waiting, the tutoring venture probably takes two hours out of the parents' day, and longer if they don't own a car. Many parents will therefore welcome your in-home service. No driving, no waiting, and one-to-one instruction for their child instead of one-to-three and, best of all, at a lower cost.

What should you charge? Phone a tutoring center and ask what they charge. That amount will serve as a guide for what you could fairly ask for your unique service.

How do you find parents who would welcome in-home tutoring for their children? Here are a few ways:

- The operators of children's stores, toy stores, or book stores might let you place a notice describing your service on their counters or in their windows. Merchants are usually eager to be of help to the community. And bookstore proprietors are particularly interested in promoting literacy.

- Doctors often see children who, among other difficulties, have a reading problem (which is sometimes the cause of the "other difficulties"). Visit their offices. If you aren't lucky enough to see the doctor, discuss your special service with the receptionist (who may have considerable clout in influencing the doctor's decision). Pediatricians constantly refer parents to our Institute — why not to your service?

- Arrange employment interviews with the operators of professional tutoring services. The bulk of their business lies in dealing with children who read poorly. You would therefore have a considerable advantage over other job-applicants, who usually have no experience in teaching reading.

- Contact operators of daycare centers and nursery schools that don't teach reading. Arrange to teach their children (dealt with in chapter 5) as a visiting specialist once or twice a week. Operators can cover the cost of your service by charging a small extra amount to those parents who want their children to receive lessons.

- Approach members of women's groups at churches, community centers, housing complexes, or even a military base, and offer either individual or group instruction for their children. If they prefer group instruction, study chapters 5 and 6.

- Suggest to librarians that you offer reading lessons on their premises — with or without library participation in the venture. Librarians are usually enthusiastic about projects that could increase their readership.

- Some public libraries have programs for mothers. Suggest to a member of the group that you will provide reading instruction for their youngsters while the parents hold their meeting.

One method of instruction that works well in teaching a number of children — as in some of the above cases — is to divide the children into groups of four or five, depending on their age and ability. Then, while the main body of children is entertained — or at least controlled — in a nearby room by one or two parents or caregivers, the first group of children receives reading instruction with blackboard demonstrations for ten minutes. They then rejoin the main group, to be replaced by the next small cluster of children. With this method, the children don't have time to become bored, and the constant rotation means each group gets two or three short lessons in the space of an hour or so. If you give parents printed material to take home, they will be able to reinforce through the week what you have taught their children.

GETTING STARTED

To illustrate the procedures, let's suppose our babysitter — we'll call her Marilyn — is sixteen, and babysits four-year-old Dermot one or two nights a week for her neighbors, Mr. and Mrs. Campbell. Marilyn therefore has an immediate potential pupil. She tells Mrs. Campbell that she has been studying how to teach reading and wonders if she might teach Dermot to read on her babysitting nights. The Campbells may be so delighted with the idea that they begin thinking about arranging more nights out, to increase the frequency of such valuable lessons.

As might be expected, Marilyn is both excited and nervous. She needed plenty of courage even to suggest the arrangement to Mrs. Campbell. But Marilyn is a spunky young lady and, having read chapter 3 (Cynthia's adventure in teaching Marcia) twice, she feels confident about meeting the challenges of her own program with Dermot.

Dermot's rapid rise to readership

Lesson 1

Because Marilyn enjoys a good relationship with Dermot, she rightly predicts that he will be an excellent pupil. After all, Dermot can't wait to be in school like the "big kids," so he appreciates Marilyn's bringing the school to him. Marilyn also plans to use the reading lessons to introduce Dermot to some of the basic discipline and restraint expected of those who attend school — which, of course, will work to her advantage. "You have to be quiet, Dermot. In school, pupils don't make noises or interrupt the teacher," (waiving, for the moment, the complete truth of the matter).

Marilyn waits until the Campbells have left before beginning Dermot's instruction; by so doing, she avoids parental observation while she gains confidence. Because Dermot is a year older than Marcia, who was described in chapter 3, Marilyn proposes to teach steps 1, 2, and 3 in the first session: **U**, **P**, and **UP**.

Dermot's lessons will be less frequent than those most parents would be able to give their children — just one or two sessions a week — so it is impractical to set up a special area in the Campbells' home with the decorative paraphernalia Cynthia employed in chapter 3. However, Mr. and Mrs. Campbell have agreed to let Marilyn affix material to the refrigerator, to the front door, and to Dermot's bedroom door. Dermot will therefore have plenty of opportunity to review the material between teaching sessions.

On the first evening of the new adventure, Marilyn arrives with the blocks game, described on pages 63 and 64 (which she constructed with a little help from her father), and the letters **U**, **P**, and **UP** in various sizes for the blocks game and for display around the home.

Marilyn wisely observes a few precautions that simplify teaching Dermot the sounds of **U**, **P**, and the word **UP**. First, she gives Dermot plenty of exercise with **U** before introducing **P**, and does this by employing some of the activities described in chapter 6 under the heading "Games for reinforcing the sound of **U**." Then, with **U** firmly established in the youngster's mind, Marilyn teaches **P**, reinforcing its learning as she did for **U**. Finally, when Dermot has learned **U** and **P** well, Marilyn uses the blocks game (with morsels of breakfast food in each cup) to fix this information in his mind and to eliminate any confusion between the two letters.

Next, Marilyn introduces Dermot to the rule of left-to-right sounding of the letters by moving his finger from left to right beneath **UP** as she sounds the letters. She does this slowly at first, then in gradually quickening sequences. As expected, Dermot doesn't immediately see that the fusion of the two letter sounds creates a word sound he knows. That will take time.

When the Campbells return home, Dermot asleep in bed, Marilyn explains what she has taught their son, and suggests they encourage him to sound the letters that are now posted around their home. She bids them goodnight and takes the blocks game away for safekeeping.

Lesson 2
Three days pass before Marilyn gets the chance to give Dermot his second lesson. When the Campbells depart, she wisely begins a review of the earlier material by engaging Dermot in some activities from lesson 1. That done, she teaches him the word **PUP** and plays the blocks game with **UP** and **PUP**. Marilyn realizes that the most important business at hand lies not in increasing the number of words Dermot can read, but in making the left-to-right sounding of the letters an automatic procedure in his mind.

Alert to the fact that it is better to err on the side of slow progress than risk confusion and loss of interest, Marilyn decides against introducing **C** and the word **CAT** this session, because Dermot seems tired. The Campbells naturally want to see quick progress. So does Marilyn. But Dermot's aptitude for learning and his attitude, temperament, and energy are the best speed-governors, and Marilyn knows that to ignore these important details is to court failure.

At this point, Marilyn has a better understanding of the challenge presented by teaching Dermot, and of her obvious skill in dealing with that challenge. By the end of the first month, Dermot is able to read **UP, PUP, CUP, CAP, TAP, CUT, HAT, HOT, HOP, POT**, and **POP**.

The Campbells, having read chapter 1 in Marilyn's copy of this book, now understand the added benefits of higher intelligence and eventual academic excellence Dermot will enjoy. Seeing that they have hit upon an educational bonanza, they arrange to be out *four* evenings a week.

The words Dermot can now read — all affixed to the refrigerator — catch the eye of neighbors Mr. and Mrs. Grabowski, who think their five-year-old daughter, Gretna, should get a similar head start in reading. They contact Marilyn, who, now experienced and confident, sets about repeating with Gretna the same simple procedures that she has so successfully employed with Dermot. Progress is even faster with the older child, despite the fact that Marilyn can devote only two nights a week to the venture. In just three weeks Gretna is able to read all the words Dermot was reading at the end of a month.

Constantly referring to chapters 2 and 3 for detailed guidance, Marilyn continues with Dermot's and Gretna's instruction on their separate nights, at a pace each child feels comfortable with.

News of Marilyn's teaching skill spreads like a ripple across the neighborhood. However, her confidence is tested to the limit when she is approached by Mr. and Mrs. Kim, who want not just one child, but two children, taught to read — and both at the same time: their daughter, Hannah, age six, and their son, Robin, age three. This isn't to be a babysitting arrangement, but a tutoring assignment, one to be conducted in the Kims' recreation room for an hour each Saturday and Sunday morning.

Unwilling to turn down the challenge, yet not knowing how to meet it, Marilyn delays her answer until she figures out how to match the quick learning ability of the older child, Hannah, with the slower learning ability of young Robin. Nothing if not resourceful, Marilyn soon hits on a solution and agrees to begin teaching the following Saturday. She quotes the Kims a fee that is one-and-a-half times the amount she would charge for just one child. The Kims agree, and Marilyn appears at their home on Saturday with the blocks game under one arm and a bag of pretzel sticks under the other.

Marilyn tactfully advises Mr. and Mrs. Kim that children usually behave differently when parents are present, and asks that she be allowed privacy while teaching the two children. The Kims agree, and Marilyn and the children proceed to the rec room.

Marilyn begins by explaining to the children that they are going to play school. She is the principal, six-year-old Hannah will be the teacher, and three-year-old Robin will be the pupil. She discusses with Hannah — with Robin looking on — what Hannah is to teach Robin: the correct sound for the letter **U**. Because Robin is watching all the time, he is alerted to what is expected of him even before Hannah attempts to teach him. The action, therefore, resembles actors rehearsing for a play.

Marilyn goes over the sound of the letter **U** repeatedly with Hannah, and shows her how to move Robin's finger around the shape while making the sound with him. Robin, observing all this, nods enthusiastically and can hardly wait to fill the role of the accommodating pupil. He is, in fact, half taught even before his big sister swings into action.

Not surprisingly, both Hannah and Robin quickly become familiar with the shape of **U** and its sound. Next, Marilyn explains to Hannah how to engage Robin in coloring **U**s in newspaper headlines with a crayon. Since Robin is witnessing the instruction, he again gets the message before his personal teacher, Hannah, bursts forth with guidance.

The following day, Sunday, after a short review of **U**, Marilyn introduces the children to **P**. When sister and brother master **P** and have played the blocks game (fueled with pretzel sticks), they read their first word, **UP**.

Before leaving, Marilyn explains the importance of review to Hannah. She urges Hannah, as teacher, to engage Robin in various forms of review — coloring **U**s and **P**s in headlines, and having him trace his finger around the large letters she has attached to the refrigerator door. By so doing, Robin will be able to move ahead with a new word (**PUP**) and a new letter (**C**) when Marilyn returns next Saturday. Hannah promises to do so.

Of course, the older child could easily move ahead more quickly were it not for her more slowly learning brother. However, the pleasure of being a teacher assures Hannah's contentment with the slower pace as the pair progresses week by week at about the same speed that Dermot has achieved.

Marilyn, now babysitting and teaching six nights a week and tutoring for an hour on Saturday and Sunday mornings, is politely refusing the additional requests for her service now coming in. But a surprise request is made, and it's one she can't refuse. One of her mother's co-workers, a good friend, Mrs. Delaney, has a son in grade 3 who can't read. Would Marilyn please, *please* help him?

With reluctance, Marilyn agrees to work her teaching magic with nine-year-old Aaron on Mondays, Wednesdays, and Fridays from 4:30 to 5:30. The teaching will have to take place at the home of Mrs. Delaney's neighbor, Mrs. Finch, who minds Aaron after school until his parents pick him up. Because the project will entail a fifteen-minute bus ride each way for Marilyn, she decides to count half of that time — fifteen minutes — as part of the tutoring time and also to add the cost of the bus tickets.

On studying chapter 7, Marilyn learns of the special difficulties that can arise when teaching a failing schoolchild. Sensing the possible need for an appealing inducement, she discusses this with Mr. and Mrs. Delaney. It takes them only a moment to hit on a suitable reward arrangement. Fascinated with magic, Aaron is a member of the magic club at school and has participated in two performances for the student body. He would like to have some high-tech magic equipment, but it's costly. Mr. and Mrs. Delancy agree to provide seventy-five dollars for the blocks game. Marilyn reasons that a dime placed in each of the blocks game receptacles will hold Aaron's attention, and that by the time he has secured his seventy-five dollars he will be reading on par with his grade 3 classmates.

To Marilyn's relief, Aaron turns out to be completely likeable. She begins by showing him the test words and sentences on page 143. The youngster is able to correctly read the words **HIS, A, IN,** and **THE,** and guesses several others, reading **cuff** as *cup*, **frost** as *fresh*, and **bud** as *bad*. Marilyn perceives that teaching Aaron isn't going to be much different from teaching her other pupils, except that she will have to curb Aaron's well formed habit of guessing.

Aaron is surprised to learn that the sounds of the letters are important in being able to read — a new notion to him — but he accepts the idea. In his first one-hour session — with six trips down the base of the blocks game for a total of $3.60 — he is able to read, without guessing, the nine words in steps 1 to 9 in chapter 2. Marilyn gives Aaron copies of the words to take home to attach to his bedroom door, and urges him to review these at least once a day.

Aaron progresses quickly, which surprises and delights not only Mr. and Mrs. Delaney, but Marilyn too. She is now pleased she undertook this originally unwanted assignment, if only for the opportunity it has given her to see the speed at which a more mature child can advance.

Aaron's reading progress continues uneventfully during each of the three-a-week lessons. While Aaron is learning, so is one other: Mrs. Finch. This lady now sees that she can offer an additional service to the parents of the other children she minds all day. Picking up a copy of this book, Mrs. Finch becomes the first caregiver in the neighborhood to provide reading instruction, and she is soon sending out her own ripples.

In time, Marilyn ends up giving Dermot, Gretna, Hannah, Robin, and Aaron a skill to which a price cannot properly be attached. They in turn end up giving her a tremendous sense of self-worth, a grand elation at having initiated so important a change in their lives, and a feeling that perhaps she has found the answer to a long-standing puzzle: what to do when she grows up. Why, of course, teach!

5

Teaching in a Daycare Center or Nursery School

Nursery schools — of which Montessori schools are probably the best known — sometimes teach reading. Daycare centers rarely do. The purpose of this chapter is to increase the effectiveness of those who already teach reading, and to show those who don't — whether at a nursery school or a daycare center — how to do so.

I discussed in chapter 1 the several benefits young children gain by being taught to read early. And, of course, those who teach them this important skill reap the immense satisfaction of having given youngsters these benefits. But there is still another dividend — a financial one — for those whose business is preschool child-minding, as Mrs. Sylvia P., of Toronto, discovered much to her surprise.

When my book *Teach Your Child to Read in 60 Days* appeared in bookstores (in 1975, long before I had a school of my own), George Halanen picked up a copy, taught his two preschoolers to read, and came up with the idea of turning the system into a boxed reading program. This, he explained, would spare parents the task of having to construct the various components described in the book. Soon the boxed program was in stores throughout North America.

Mrs. P. — who operated both a daycare center and a nursery school — had always believed that preschool education lacked adequate intellectual stimulation. She bought the boxed kit and began to teach reading at her two establishments. Then, the surprise.

Word of Mrs. P.'s innovative reading instruction program attracted the media. Her adventure was featured in the newspaper. Still more impressive, Mrs. P. was asked to appear on *two* national TV talk shows to describe her success in teaching preschoolers to read. What effect do you suppose all this publicity had on Mrs. P.'s business?

There's no guarantee that the introduction of a reading program to your center will land you on TV. But I can guarantee one thing: if you introduce reading instruction at your school or center, parents will spread the word about the superior service you are providing. Given a choice between sending their child to a center that teaches reading, and one that doesn't, which center are parents likely to choose? Which would *you* choose?

At a for-profit child center the decision to begin a reading program will rest mainly with the owner-operator. However, at a non-profit or co-op center the decision will probably be divided between the professionally trained staff and the parents with whom they maintain a close working relationship.

YOU CAN DO IT!

What special ability do you need to begin a reading program? Just the ability you already have: the ability to manage a group of children and win their cooperation. The step-by-step system presented in chapter 2 provides all the information you need. Learn it and you will be ready to begin.

Is nothing more needed? Well, yes, one thing that I was saving to the last — *confidence.* You probably know that Tarzan places one foot on the prostrate body of each defeated assailant, then thumps his chest, and bellows loudly in celebration of his great power. This generates a flow of adrenaline and sets him up to waste the next unwise challenger (though with all due respect to Tarzan, he never faced a group of preschoolers). You get the picture. And if a modest amount of figurative chest-thumping will start the "can-do" juices swirling through your arteries, then beat away. You can do it! Take heart in knowing that if you have fewer than twelve children per caregiver or teacher at your center, you have a major advantage over teachers at the Institute.*

You have another important advantage. Parents whose children attend the Institute expect to see impressive reading advancement — our reputation is based on it. So, in ten months our two- and three-year-olds have usually completed a *Primer* and have advanced to a *First Reader*. But you have no such commitment or obligation. If your children merely learn to read a few simple words and sentences — as Mrs. P.'s did — parents will hail this as marvelous.

And it *will* be marvelous, because even this introductory level of reading will indoctrinate children in the vitally important reading ritual (described in part 1 — The Phonic Reading Method). Moreover, you will have contributed greatly to the children's intellectual and academic advancement.

Though various teaching procedures will be described, you needn't use all of them nor achieve spectacular results. Pick and choose from the methods, and get started. You will soon be collecting compliments from parents. Of greater importance, you will have the satisfaction of knowing that much of the magic you work will be taking place — unseen — in children's heads. It will represent your personal contribution to the success of children you have loved and whose lives you have briefly touched.

PLANNING YOUR PROGRAM

Before beginning your program, alert parents to your plan. Describe the various advantages (detailed in chapter 1) their children will receive. Perhaps invite parents to a special late-afternoon meeting and describe the project. What will you say? Just express the thoughts

---

* In Ontario, the maximum legal teacher-pupil ratio in nursery schools and daycare centers for children between the ages of two-and-a-half and five years is eight children per caregiver, but this ratio doesn't apply to private schools, where classes can be larger.

conveyed in chapter 1, or simply read aloud the text in that chapter under the heading "Of what value is reading ability to a preschooler?"

The chapters for teaching a preschooler (chapter 3) and for school-teachers (chapter 6) describe many procedures you can use either in their present form or with slight alteration. As with any teaching activity, half the battle lies in keeping the children entertained, so numerous playful activities are described to help you keep them amused.

Let's consider still other activities suited for working with small groups of children. You might begin with the ledge game.

Construction of the ledge game

You will need

- a sheet of 3/4-inch plywood (or some composite wood material) 122 by 81 centimeters (48 by 32 inches);
- three 122-centimeter (48-inch) lengths of one-inch quarter-round (to make the ledges);
- ten pieces of heavy cardboard or Masonite about 23 centimeters (9 inches) square, and four pieces 23 by 33 centimeters (9 by 13 inches); and
- six large photos of animals to attach to the cardboard squares. (Calendars are a good source of large animal photos.)

Affix the six large animal photos to six of the cardboard squares. Enlarge on a photocopier or print by hand the first few letters and words up to step 7 in chapter 3: **U, P, C, A, UP, PUP, CUP,** and **CAP.** Affix these to cardboard pieces as you did the animal photos, the four letters going on square pieces and the four words going on the rectangular pieces.

Attach the three pieces of quarter-round lengthwise along the sheet of plywood so as to provide three long ledges (see figure 13). Attach the plywood sheet to a wall on a slight slant so the cardboard plaques won't tip off.

Figure 13: Set-up for the ledge game

The general set-up for the ledge game, seen in figure 13, shows an advanced stage of play, with the first five plaques now in the game. But let's start at the beginning.

Playing the ledge game

Teach the sound of **U** by employing any of the techniques described in chapters 3 and 6. Then, when all the children can sound the letter correctly — possibly in a few days' time — have the group sit on the floor facing the ledge game. Place the letter **U** on the right side of one of the animals.

Let's say the letter **U** is positioned to the right of the dog. You might begin by saying, "The bear would like *uh*." Choose a child to approach the ledge unit and wipe a finger beneath the **U** *from left to right* (this is important) while sounding the letter **U** (*uh*). The child then moves the **U**-plaque and places it on the right side of the bear.

Repeat the procedure by having another child move the letter to the right side of some other animal that is supposedly requesting it. By engaging children in this ritual for five minutes in the morning (and, if you wish, another five minutes in the afternoon) your group will soon be familiar with the letter shape **U** and its sound. Proceed slowly. *Don't rush.* A slow, comfortable start will avoid confusion and build your children's confidence.

When all your children can sound the **U** correctly and understand the workings of the ledge game, teach the letter **P** in the same way you taught them **U**. When they can all make the correct sound for **P**, include it in the ledge game with **U**.

When children feel comfortable working with **U** and **P**, teach them the word **UP**, and include **UP** in the ledge game, playing now with **U**, **P**, and **UP**. When a child moves the word plaque **UP** to the requested new position, he or she runs a finger beneath the letters while sounding each of them, and then wipes a finger once again *from left to right* beneath the two letters, saying, "Up."

Don't expect children to notice that the combined sounds of *uh* and *Puh* form the spoken word *up*. Even if you point out this detail to them, young children are unlikely to understand the wondrous effect being produced. In time — a few weeks, perhaps — your youngsters will see the connection. Don't attempt to rush it.

When the next plaque, **CUP**, is added to the game, one of the other plaques — perhaps **U** — will be removed from the game. There can be no more than five letters or words in play at a time. The photo below shows the ledge game in progress.

The ledge game in progress

The plaque game

When the children have learned a few letters and words, the plaques can be used for another procedure. For this second use, print or write on the back of each plaque the letter or word that is on the opposite side. If the plaque contains a word rather than a single letter, place marks on the bottom edge of the back to indicate the middle of each letter in the word.

Now, sit facing the group with the stack of letters and words face-down on your lap. Hold up the first plaque and run your finger from right to left (which would appear to the children as left to right) beneath the letter or each letter in the word and sound the letter(s) for them. (The purpose of the marks along the bottom edge is so you won't have to twist your head around the front of the plaque to see if your finger is directly beneath a letter.) Or, you might instead position your finger beneath the letters in a word and ask children to sound them. We used this simple procedure for years before finally creating a *Primer* to replace the stacking of plaques.

If you are teaching one child at a time, rather than a group, have the child sit facing a wall or something that impedes a view of the classroom (so he or she won't be distracted by other activities going on). And, because children's eyes often stray to the teacher's face instead of looking at the plaques, you might sit behind the child and bring each plaque around into his or her view.

Playdough boards

If you coat the plaques with clear urethane or lacquer, or some other durable sealant, they can also be used for a seat activity. Children can position dots of playdough around the shapes of the letters, thus fixing each shape more firmly in their minds.

Repetition is, of course, the key to quick progress, and an activity that invites much repetition is the train game.

The train game

To prepare the train game, draw a train engine — or a wagon, or boat, or any vehicle you choose. Make photocopies of your drawing. On the side of each engine, print a letter or word of your choice. Then the photocopies can either be folded to stand upright like tents, or trimmed and glued to wooden blocks — as has been done in the photo on page 103. Three tents or blocks are used in the game.

The train game is suitable for teaching two or three children at a time. However, the exercise can easily be used for more children if the engines are made larger and the ritual performed on a ledge — perhaps a chalk ledge — on the wall.

To play the game, the first child sounds the letter — or the letters in a word — on the front engine, then sounds those on the second engine, then finally on the third engine. Next, the child moves the third engine ahead of the other two engines and begins again to

The train game in progress

sound letters and read words on the first engine, the second, and the third. Then it's the next child's turn to follow the same procedure, a procedure that obviously will move the procession of three engines slowly along the table or ledge. You might set up some small item to serve as a train station toward which the engines will slowly move.

Tracing

Make a series of dots with a pen to create large versions of the letters and words the children are learning at the moment. Photocopied, these will provide a valuable exercise in tracing, one that not only reinforces the letter shapes in children's minds, but also provides valuable exercise in using a writing tool: a preparation for eventual printing and writing. When sent home, the tracings will remind parents of your efforts and dedication to their children's advancement.

See chapter 6 for more ideas about material to send home. Also in that chapter you will find additional games to use either in the way they are presented or in a simplified form.

THE READING RECORD BOOK

If you want to keep parents informed about their child's reading progress, you could introduce something similar to the reading record book described on pages 122 and 123. The book serves a three-fold purpose: first, by reporting briefly on a child's reading activity each day; second, by encouraging parental involvement in their child's reading advancement; and third, by helping to secure children's cooperation in working with parents.

How do you secure parental help? You might insert in the reading record book a message to parents, similar to that which we place at the front of our reading record books.

The Reading Record Book

Learning to read is too wonderful and important an occasion in a child's life to be left entirely to those outside the family for its accomplishment. That's why we invite parents to participate in their child's reading advancement at home, and we provide parents with special materials to help them win their child's cooperation.

And, of course, when you participate at home, your child will advance in reading more easily and quickly.

Your child will bring this book home each day. In it, your child's teacher will describe briefly what your child has read at school. You will then know what he or she should read for you at home — perhaps during a few minutes before supper, or after supper, or even before "lights out." You can then indicate, in the space provided, that your child has read this same material for you. Then, when your child brings the book back to school, the teacher, seeing that your child has cooperated with you, will insert a sticker in the space above your remarks.

But note: The purpose of home reading is to give children practice with what they have already learned, not to push ahead with new material. And note equally: pushing children ahead too quickly invites confusion, and when children become confused, they lose interest.

Another valuable purpose of this book is to provide you with a permanent record of your child's rise to literacy and of the important part you played in that adventure: a record that you and your child may treasure in the years ahead.

Tips on Motivating Your Child

If your child is always willing to read for you, fine. Sometimes, though, children are more interested in reading to a parent when they, not the parent, think of it. If this is sometimes the case in your home, you might leave small reminders of reading around the home. For example, you could leave this book open somewhere as a reminder of the stickers already earned and of the blank spaces still to be filled. If these stratagems don't work, you could remind your child of reading — but in an apparently unconcerned way: "I wonder what sticker you'll get in your book tomorrow, Hannibal." Or you might actually suggest that your child read, but not in a direct way. In many homes the question, "Shall we read for a little while?" might secure a prompt *no*. Better if you say, "Hey, maybe we should get busy and earn another sticker to show Grandma (or your spouse, or a friend, or just teddy bear)."

Tactful guidance of this sort may be necessary only until your child begins to enjoy the magic of print and can decipher it easily. When that point is reached, your youngster will beg you to help him or her read at every opportunity.

If you think daily reports in a reading record book would be too time-consuming, you might send home a report just once or twice a week. Or send home no report at all — heroic effort isn't needed to win parents' respect and appreciation. If you accomplish no more than to teach children the basics of reading — to sound letters correctly, and in a left-to-right direction — and teach them to read a few dozen words, you will still have made a commendable contribution to their eventual academic performance.

However, if you can continue to step 32, your children will be reading about a hundred words and will be ready to begin reading sentences, dealt with in chapter 8. Parents will be *very* impressed.

6

Kindergarten and Grade 1 Teachers

When media cannons blast public schooling for the prevalence of illiteracy, their sights often settle on teachers. What simpler explanation for reading failures can there be than unskilled teaching? School psychologists then rally in defence of teachers, and launch blame for poor reading at parents, with charges of unconcern and adverse influences in the home: unrestricted TV viewing, parental strife, sibling rivalry, and other domestic horrors. The resultant picture is that, between them, schoolteachers and parents form a sort of Laurel and Hardy team of incompetents who are ruining a good educational system. This could be swallowed whole only if we were to ignore a third element: the educational bureaucracy — with whom I had a memorable encounter.

Thinking I might help public schools increase their success in teaching reading, I presented plans, separately, to the educational directors of three cities within Metropolitan Toronto for a reading program that would permit public school teachers to achieve the same one hundred percent success my own teachers achieve with two- and three-year-olds.

The basic system had already been devised, tested, and proved. The procedures that were completely effective at my school for teaching groups of younger children were easily altered for groups of mature pupils. Because of the attention that had been directed to our school by the media, plus the popularity of my books, my activities in the field of reading were reasonably well known.

How did the directors of education react to my proposal? They weren't interested.

Here was a complacency that has escaped media notice, and I pondered with renewed reverence B. F. Skinner's sage conclusion that public education isn't likely to improve, because no heads will roll if it *doesn't* improve. My respect and sympathy for schoolteachers rose sharply, and I marveled that they perform as well as they do with unenterprising leadership.

The sad extent of bureaucratic contrariness and ineptitude in educational management is told by former U.S. Secretary of Education William J. Bennett, in his book *The De-Valuing of America* (Summit Books, 1992): a chilling report on the whole iceberg of educational malpractice, of which my chance encounter was but the tip.

Enough said of the matter. The purpose of this chapter is to give teachers of reading the knowledge and guidance they aren't likely to get through establishment channels.

FAULTY READING SYSTEMS IN THE SCHOOLS

The whole language reading method is used in many classrooms today. I discussed in chapter 1 why this system is inferior to the phonic method. The whole language method is, in fact, merely a rehash of the faulty look-say or whole word method popular forty years ago: basal reading programs that are essentially untested.

Hold it. Did I say *untested*? Yes, Allen Barton and David Wilder, who conducted the Columbia Reading Study, asked creators of basal (whole word) reading programs whether the guidance given in the teachers' handbooks was based on "definite scientific proof" — in other words, had anyone ever bothered to test the material and

procedures on children? Most of the experts responsible for produc-
ing the basals said "No."*

The awesome picture that emerges is one of supposed experts —
who we can't be sure ever taught a child to read — telling teachers
what they *think* might work! Risking professional censure, I'd say
there's material here for a TV sitcom.

Assuredly, many children eventually learn to read with the whole language basal programs, but many others end up functionally illiterate,
unable, that is, to read simple text. Still others become *scholastically illiterate*, meaning they can labor through a sentence or paragraph, but
with such difficulty that they gain only a hazy understanding of what
the writer wanted to convey. These stumblers are nevertheless called
readers; however, their academic prospects are greatly compromised,
and they have no future in any field that requires fluent reading ability.

Unfortunately, children don't fall neatly into easily identifiable
categories of functional illiterates, or scholastic illiterates, or skilful
readers. We will never know to what extent the ability of seemingly
good readers has been degraded, or to what extent they have been
adversely disposed to reading by a program that made this simple skill
unnecessarily difficult.

Often, when whole word and whole language methods have seemed
to chalk up moments of triumph, it is because teachers deceitfully traf-
ficked in what is known as "bootleg phonics." In other words, they
engaged in illicit teaching of the forbidden letter sounds when their
superiors weren't around. Additionally, many children were smart
enough to figure out — without their teacher's help — the connection
that exists between letters and letter-sounds.

But many children were, and still are, unable to understand
the phonic letter code without explicit and repeated instruction in the
procedure, plus plenty of practice in using that knowledge to puzzle
out the identity of words. These children (often termed dyslexic or
learning disadvantaged by the experts) are the ones we deal with at
our reading clinic. After only a few hours of letter sound instruction,
the same children become skilful and adventurous readers. Their

---

* Jeanne Chall, *Learning to Read: The Great Debate* (McGraw-Hill, 1983).

reading vocabularies expand with ever increasing acceleration as they gradually master the sound code represented by letters and letter combinations.

YOUR CLASS WILL BECOME READERS

Whether you teach kindergarten or grade 1, the instructions that follow will permit you to advance your pupils from illiteracy to literacy by the end of a ten-month school year. Kindergarten teachers may need some reassuring about this because the traditional mindset of educational authorities is one of low expectancy for five-year-olds. The popular notion is that the five-year-old mind is incapable of dealing with anything more complex than cutting and gluing shapes, stringing beads, and so on. Reading? Faint hope, or impossible.

Let me apply some judo leverage to your thinking. My preschool teachers' hearts would float like butterflies at the prospect of teaching children as old as five to read. Five-year-olds possess levels of understanding, memory, and often, interest, plus attention spans, never encountered when teaching two- and three-year-olds. Even teaching a four-year-old is heralded as a big break. Having said this, though, one easily understands the apprehension kindergarten teachers might feel about treading where none (or few) have trodden before. Take heart. Don't be overwhelmed. You have here a program specifically designed *and tested* for your task. Look in the mirror and see a winner.

PLANNING YOUR PROGRAM

Not many teachers may want to limit their reading instruction to the ten minutes a day that youngsters at my school receive. Still, you are the best judge of how much time you can comfortably devote to reading instruction each day. Keep in mind, though, that — as stated in the introduction to part 2 — it is the *number* of recalls that speeds learning, and that several short sessions will be more effective than a few longer ones.

Before beginning your program, read chapter 3, "Teaching a Preschooler," if you haven't already done so, and chapter 5, where you will find games suitable for your use in their present form or with slight alteration. The procedures described in these chapters can also help steer your thinking along lines that will trigger your own creative thoughts. And, of course, the steps presented in chapter 2 must be mastered before you begin your program.

There are roughly 170 to 180 school days in the year, depending on the number of days set aside by school administrators for professional advancement and holidays. This allows plenty of time for you to have your children reading skilfully in just one school year. By beginning with a slow rate of progress (there's no need to hurry), your class will be reading more than a hundred words long before Christmas.

I have provided a sample schedule for you to use as a reference. The schedule features a relaxed speed of advancement, slow enough to permit the less able children in your class (or those who fall behind because of absence) to keep up with the others. The use of games and nonsense lets you accommodate the needs of those who progress slowly, and to do so in a way that won't bore the others. The numbers in the schedule indicate the approximate progression of school days.

You will see that pupils learn only two letter sounds and two words in the first five days. But, of greater importance, they will be learning a *system*, one so valuable that we don't want to rush the procedure and risk confusion.

Notice also that no more than one new piece of information is introduced at a time, and on days when several words are introduced, all elements of those words have already been taught.

Step	Day	Content
1	1	U
2	2	P
3	3, 4, 5	UP, PUP
4	6	C
5	7	CUP
6	8	A

Step	Day	Content
7	9	CAP
	10	review
8	11	T
9	12, 13	AT, PAT, CAT, TAP, CUT
10	14	the
11	15	H
12	16	HAT
13	17	O
14	18, 19, 20	HOT, HOP, TOP, POP, POT, COT, COP
15	21	G
16	22	HUG, GOT, TAG, TUG, HOG, GAG, GAP
17	23	B
18	24	BAG, BAT, BUG, TUB, CUB, CAB, COB, BOB, BUT
19, 20	25	thAT, I
21	26	PIG, BIT, HIT, TIP, HIP, BIB, BIG
22	27	R
23a	28	RAT, RUG, RUB, ROB, RAG, RIP, RIB
23b	29	TRIP, TRAP, GRAB, CRIB, CRAB, BRAG
	30	review
24	31	N
25	32, 33	IN, ON, ANT, PIN, PAN, RUN, RAN, CAN, NOT, BUN, GUN, TIN, NUT, NIP, NAP, HANG, BANG, RING, RUNG
26	34	S
27a	35	SIT, SAT, BUS, SUN, GAS, PASS, RUST, STOP, SPIN
27b	36	SONG, SING, SANG, STUNT, STRING, STRONG, PANTS, CATS, POTS, CUPS
28	37	thIS
29	38	D

Step	Day	Content
30	39, 40	DOG, DIG, HID, DOT, ADD, BAD, PAD, AND, HAND, SAND, BAND, DRIP, DROP, DRAG
31	41	E
32	42, 43	RED, HEN, PEN, TEN, BED, BEG, BET, PET, NET, RENT, STEP, NEST, PEST, BEST, REST

Teaching the above 127 words in forty-three days means you will be ready to move ahead with sentences in the first or second week of November. This, then, is the rough plan. But first there is an important introductory procedure.

GETTING STARTED: LETTER SOUNDS

You are now ready to introduce your class to the wonders of reading. But first you need to sensitize their ears to the sounds of letters as they occur in speech. As discussed in chapter 2, the easiest letter sounds for children to isolate are for letters that occur at the beginning of words. This presents no challenge to adults, but it is a major task in detection for children who haven't had to think about speech sounds before. Because the first three letters to be taught are **U**, **P**, and **C**, we'll start with them. But, at this early stage *don't* show these letters on the board. For the moment, we are concerned only with letter *sounds*, not with letter appearance.

Begin by asking pupils if they can think of any words that begin with an **uh** sound. You may have to suggest some words suitable for children this age: *up, uncle, under, ugly, uncover, understand, undress, unfold, unfriendly, unhappy, unhealthy, unsafe, untangle, untidy, until, untrue, unwrap, upset*. Again, *don't* show these words on the board — our exercise deals only with sound.

Next, ask the class if anyone can think of words that start with a **P**uh sound, which might bring a response (but don't count on it) of *pot*, *pop, popcorn, pony,* and several other words, including names such as *Peter, Paul,* and *Patricia.* Don't show either the letter or the words on the board. We are concerned only with sound.

Finally, ask if anyone can think of words beginning with the sound *Cuh* — and because we're dealing only with sound, not the appearance of a letter, it won't matter if children suggest words that start with a *K.* So, for this activity, words such as *keep, kick,* and *kangaroo* will be as acceptable in the game as *cookie, candy,* and *corn.* Again, don't show these letters or words on the board.

When the class has engaged in the above exercises with **uh**, **Puh**, and **Cuh**, play the following game to speed the children's perception and understanding of beginning sounds.

The Beginning-sound game

Have five children stand on each side of the room. You then sound **uh**, **Puh**, or **Cuh** and name one of the children. He or she must say a word that begins with that sound and then name a child on the opposing team. That other child must now say a word that begins with the same sound before naming a child on the other team. And so it goes, back and forth, until a child is stuck. The player who is stuck or who says a word starting with the wrong sound sits down. Then voice one of the two remaining sounds, and name a child to say a word beginning with that sound. The game continues as before until a child is stuck. Eventually, only one child is left: the winner. The only rule to establish is that once a word has been spoken, it can't be used again in the same game.

Now we begin to introduce the letter shapes and match the correct sound to each.

Day 1: Step 1

Today we teach the letter **U** — and no more. When you teach children just one letter sound, they can't confuse it with any other; it takes an alternative to breed confusion. Of course, some children will already know this letter as *yoo,* so we already have the genesis of confusion, but it's a confusion we'll erase with a highly repetitive teaching procedure. The more effectively we teach children the sound of **U** (as described

on page 37) and its letter shape, the less chance there will be of confusion arising when we introduce subsequent letters. Begin by chalking
a large U on the board and making the special *uh* sound several times
for the class, inviting them to repeat the sound along with you. Make
sure your pupils s-t-r-e-t-c-h their mouths appropriately to make a good
distinctive sound — a sound that won't ultimately be confused with the
sounds of other vowels when they are introduced.

Games for reinforcing the sound of U
It will become obvious that most of the following games can be
adapted to each new letter you eventually introduce. So, the value of
each game described exceeds its mere reinforcement of the letter U.

1. By raising your hands and slightly bending your elbows, show the
   class how you can form the general shape of U with your arms. Have
   the class stand, raise their arms similarly, and repeat *uh* in a spaced
   chant.
2. With your hands raised, sing an *uh* song and see who can identify it.
   For example, you might give voice to the notes of "Happy Birthday
   to You" or some other well-known song by sounding each note with
   an *uh*.
3. Have a contest. Who can raise their hands and balance on one foot
   while saying *uh* repeatedly? For how long? How about hopping on
   that foot?
4. Who can say *uh* and stretch that sound for the longest time?
5. Hold a relay race. Print a large U at extreme ends of a chalkboard
   or affix two printed letters some distance apart. Line up a team of
   six players beside each of the two Us. On the word, "Go," the first
   member of each team runs to the far U, touches it, sounds *uh*,
   then runs back to touch the hand of the next player on his or
   her team, who then repeats the procedure. And so it goes on until
   the fastest team wins. The game might also be made an outdoor
   activity.
6. Pupils who are having difficulty making or remembering the
   correct sound should come to the front of the room to engage
   in a bouncing ball contest. Pupils take turns bouncing the ball — a

basketball or a sponge-rubber ball — as quickly as they can (by gradually moving their ball-bouncing hand closer to the floor) and voicing the letter sound with each bounce.

7. Hold a "think of a game, contest, or competition" session. Pupils might come up with a few good ideas, or ideas that become good when modified slightly.

8. Nonsense and humor are powerful forces for snaring and maintaining children's attention and interest. One effective ruse is to wait until they've busied themselves with matters other than reading, then say, "I'm going to put something on the board that is very difficult to remember and which you've probably all forgotten." Then draw a **U**. See them glow with pride and radiate smug smiles — despite the absurdity of it all — when they prove you are wrong. Whirl around in mock surprise and they will love it.

9. When you want a quiet moment to attend to other tasks, distribute to each pupil a printed sheet bearing text in capital letters — newspaper headlines, flyers, any form of advertisement — and ask pupils to circle any **U**s they can find. If some youngsters have too primitive a control of the pencil to make a circle, they could scratch a mark or color the space between the upright arms of each **U**.

Create a series of sheets featuring each new letter (and eventually words) twenty-five or thirty centimeters (ten or twelve inches) high, and thus easily seen at the back of the classroom. (Use a sans serif font such as Helvetica, Futura, or Franklin Gothic.) Affix copies of the letter being learned — **U** for the moment — to the wall in various locations around the classroom (in the same way that parents are advised, in chapter 4, to display letters around the home).

Reading reinforcement at home

We want your pupils to see the letter **U** as often as possible, not only in the classroom, but in as many ways as we can arrange. Most parents will honor a request for a small amount of help — such as attaching a piece of paper to the refrigerator door — and there is great value to be reaped from even this small contribution. Figure 14 shows a tracing exercise for pupils that helps fix the **U** more firmly in their minds.

The accompanying text asks parents to post the sheet somewhere in the home.

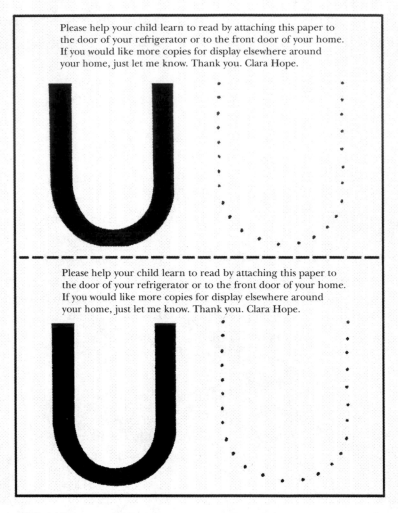

Figure 14: Invoking parental help

Day 2: Step 2

Begin by reviewing **U**, using any of the games you played yesterday, perhaps even introducing a new one. Then introduce **P**, the sound of which, when correctly made, won't carry well in a large room — so give plenty of explosive force *without voice* to your sounding. Move around the classroom, if necessary, making the sound for each row or table. Here are two ways you might exercise children in making the sound of **P** correctly.

1. Light a candle. Have children take turns, standing or sitting at a pre-scribed distance from the candle, giving as much explosive power as they can to their sounding of *Puh*, to try to blow out the candle. If the distance between the children's mouths and the candle makes extinction difficult, you'll spend less time striking matches.
2. Cement a ping-pong ball or tie a balloon to one end of a piece of string. Suspend the object in some manner, perhaps by affixing the other end of the string to the wall or to the chalkboard. Pupils stand on a prescribed spot and, sounding *Puh* with all their might, see how far they can deflect the ball or balloon from its resting position. The point to which each child manages to deflect the object is chalked on the board.

Distinguishing between the letters

Now that the children have learned two letter sounds, you would be wise to sharpen their ability to distinguish between them. The follow-ing simple procedure is one you might use as each new letter is introduced. Chalk a number of large **U**s and **P**s on the board in a mixed-up manner, then ask someone what letter he or she would like to have erased. On learning the choice — say, a **P** — you might point to a **U** asking, "This one?" and get a chorus of corrections. Erasing a **P**, you would then ask another child for his or her preferred erasure. And so it goes until the board is clear of letters. Sheer nonsense. But the nonsense fastens all eyes on the procedure, and in doing so, max-imizes your teaching efficiency. You could as easily draw an immense tree and "hang" the letters from its foliage, or draw a large blimp and print the letters on its side.

Finally:

1. distribute newspaper headlines or other printed matter so children can now mark both **U**s and **P**s, and
2. send home a tracing slip for **P**, similar to the one you sent for **U**, for the parent to attach to the refrigerator door.

These two procedures should be followed with every new letter introduced from now on, though the procedures won't be mentioned again.

Day 3: Step 3

Today, the children learn to read their first word. Well, *some* children
will. Many of the children may already have a "sight" (whole word)
reading vocabulary that includes **STOP** (from street signs) and words
that appear frequently on TV or cereal boxes. But this may be the first
time even these children learn that it matters on which side of a word
one begins reading, and that the reason for beginning on the left side
is because the first squiggle in **STOP** — for example — has an important connection with the first sound we make when we speak the word.

Introducing children to the left-to-right reading procedure — a
ritual you and I have employed with every word we've ever read (consequently, millions of times) — is of greater importance than reading
the word **UP**. However, avoid using the words *left* and *right* in your
teaching. Some children may not understand the terms, and this isn't
the time to be teaching extraneous matters. The phrases *on this side*
and *not that side* will be understood by all. To help indoctrinate
children in the left-to-right ritual, print on the chalkboard or on sheets
of paper attached to the wall or chalkboard — or otherwise display —
U, **P**, and **UP** and sound out all three. Always draw your finger from
left to right beneath any letter you are sounding or any word you are
reading. To help fix this procedure in the children's minds quickly
play the left-to-right game.

The left-to-right game

Divide your class into teams — perhaps four teams of eight children
each. Have children form four lines facing the chalkboard: teams 1, 2,
3, and 4. **U**, **P**, and **UP** should be positioned sufficiently high to be
seen over the head of any child who stands in front of them.

On the word, "Go," the child at the head of team 1 steps up to the
chalkboard and runs a finger beneath the **U** from left to right, while
sounding it *uh*, then runs a finger beneath the **P** from left to right,
sounding it *Puh*, moves to the **UP**, runs a finger beneath the word
from left to right, sounding *uh*, *Puh*, and then says the word *up*.

As soon as the first child says, "Up," the child at the head of team 2 quickly steps up to the board and repeats the sounding out and reading ritual (while the child from team 1 is taking a position at the rear of team 1). The game proceeds in this manner with children from teams 3 and 4 sounding the letters and reading the word.

Fun and excitement is generated by setting a kitchen timer to ring and placing it in a bag (so no one can see how close it is to ringing). When the timer rings, the child who is standing at the chalkboard — or is about to start sounding the letters — is eliminated from the game. Setting the timer for short periods — say, between thirty and seventy-five seconds — will add to the excitement.

A running commentary by you — as if for a horse race — will promote fidgety excitement among the team members. You might also add interest to the game by giving the teams names: Tigers, Cheetahs, Gazelles, and so on, though the children themselves may suggest preferred names.

Send home slips featuring the word **UP** in printing and in tracing format (see figure 15).

Figure 15: Invoking parental help

Day 4: Step 3 continued

Today, the children will learn that the position of letters isn't fixed or immutable, but that they can be moved around to fit our need. And our need, at this moment, is the word **PUP**. However, begin with a review (which should become a daily ritual) — in this case, a review of **UP**. That accomplished, show the class the magical transformation that takes place to **UP** when **P** is placed in front of it to form **PUP**. Then proceed with a familiarization and sounding out procedure with **PUP** similar to the one you used with **UP**.

Day 5: Review

This is a review day, one that will help ensure that all your children fully understand the letter sounds as well as the all-important basic left-to-right reading ritual. Never forget that you and I have employed the left-to-right reading ritual millions of times (about 50,000 times just in reading a book as thick as this one), and until children have employed the same procedure at least a few hundred times they are likely to slip up occasionally. Today, then, we review **U**, **P**, **UP**, and **PUP**. Play the left-to-right game and any of the other games that will help diminish confusion in the children's minds about what they have now learned.

The supreme dunce as teacher

If, while you are working at the chalkboard, you fit a puppet onto one hand and have it fill the role of a know-it-all dunce, you will have a means of introducing considerable entertainment to your teaching. Furthermore, the comic dunce will let you repeat letter sounds far more often than your children would otherwise tolerate.

Some teachers may think, *Oh, knowing it's me speaking, and not the puppet, they won't have any interest in that gag.* You'll be surprised. Consider this: I began taking a dummy mouse (of the sort sold in pet stores) into the preschool classrooms (the two- and three-year-olds). Cupping the mouse in my hands and grasping its tail between two unseen fingers, I make the mouse's head wiggle and dart in and out between my fingers. The children then line up to touch the mouse's nose. Then the four- and five-year-old kindergartners began asking to see the mouse perform. But I was really surprised when the grade 1 to 4 children began asking to see the mouse caper — and these are exceptionally bright children. Most, if not all, of them either know or suspect the mouse is a dummy (I remain noncommittal when asked), but they enjoy the farce anyway, *day after day*. I am possibly one of few school directors who, on entering classrooms, is greeted with, "Where's the mouse?"

The point is that children welcome entertainment so highly that they will reduce their need for credibility so as to make the entertainment acceptable. And they will do the same for you and your puppet. The puppet is an ever ready teaching ally that can work to your advantage by bragging and demanding to take over the instruction of the class, mixing everything up, and then concocting elaborate excuses to explain its every failing.

The mechanics are simple. When the puppet is supposed to be speaking, turn your head toward the puppet. Children will follow your gaze. And when you are supposed to be speaking, turn your head toward the class. Take courage. You can do it. What's more, the children *want* you to do it. It's show biz, yes. But nonsense can be a powerful teaching ally.

In passing, we might nod respectfully toward that early champion of playful teaching, the English philosopher John Locke, who wrote three hundred years ago:

> *I have always had a fancy that learning might be made a play and recreation to children; and that they might be brought to desire to be taught if it were proposed to them as a thing of honor, credit, delight, and recreation, or as a reward for doing something else.* *

The playful methods used for teaching a preschooler in chapter 3 are to some extent applicable to your situation, because some children in your class may have no more aptitude for learning than the fictitious three-year-old Marcia. So, some of the suggestions made in that chapter might serve you equally well.

---

* John Locke, *Some Thoughts Concerning Education* (New York, 1964).

The thundering velvet glove

The fun generated by playing the various games adds up to a new disciplinary power for your arsenal of restraints. "OK, Hector, if I have to speak to you again, you miss the reading game this afternoon. Get my message?" Not a great teaching loss for you, because the child will still witness the activities and learn from them, even though barred from participating.

Day 6: Step 4

We introduce the letter **C** today, giving it the special *Cuh* sound as described on page 41 — a sound without voice, just air. When all the children can make the new sound correctly, proceed with memory-fixing repetition using any of the games on pages 114–115, or try something even sillier. Have four or five children at a time stand at the front of the class and repeat *Cuh* for ten seconds while blinking their eyes and flapping their arms in an attempt to fly. Have successive groups repeat the procedure. Because this is the only new piece of information for the day, you might use the same absurd routine for a review of **uh**, **P***uh*, *up*, and **P***uh*, **uh**, **P***uh*, *pup*.

Day 7: Step 5

Today, children learn to sound and say **CUP** — "*Cuh*, **uh**, **P***uh*, *cup*." Having printed this on the chalkboard high enough to be seen over children's heads, invite pupils to the front to run a finger beneath the letters, and then speak the word. Then play the left-to-right game with **U**, **P**, **C**, **UP**, **PUP**, and **CUP**.

Day 8: Step 6

Teach children the sound for **A** (as described on page 44), and when they have mastered the sound, hold an "ugly contest." Ask children to come to the front, stand beneath an immense **A** on the chalkboard, stick their fingers in their ears, make a horrible face, and sound **A** five times. There might be several winners to the contest.

Reporting to parents

Dealing with a maximum of just twelve children, my teachers have time to send home a brief (five- or six-word) daily report on each child's reading activity (remember that each child in the group is reading at a different level). Teachers record their comments in a book called the Reading Record Book — a folder containing specially prepared sheets (figure 16). By such means, parents are kept informed of their child's progress and of what material to review with their child that evening. If the child cooperates with the parent in reviewing the material, the parent indicates this by initialing a designated place. The next day, noting that the child worked with the parent, the teacher places a sticker in the book as a reward for the child's cooperation at home. (See sample on page 124. The reading record book is further described starting on page 104.)

Such a daily ritual could be difficult to perform with a large class. However, a weekly report might be worth your consideration for the simple reason that every parent who reinforces your effort is almost as good as a helper in your classroom.

Day 9: Step 7
The word for today is **CAP** — *Cuh, A, Puh, cap*. Follow the same procedures as for day 7.

Day 10: Review
Today is given over to review. Nothing is lost by making sure everyone in the class has a solid understanding of everything that has gone before. By ensuring expertise at this early stage you help to ensure quick progress later. The left-to-right game will promote repetition. You might like to accompany this procedure with another game:

The famous person TV reading show
To begin, ask the class for the names of people they regard as being famous — movie stars, sports figures, singers, TV personalities, and so on. Make a list of the names but don't let the class see the names in print because of the conflicting sounds often given to the letters in people's names (dealt with on page 47). Select ten pupils — each pupil is to fill the role of one of the famous people. It doesn't matter that most of the class will forget which child represents whom. The

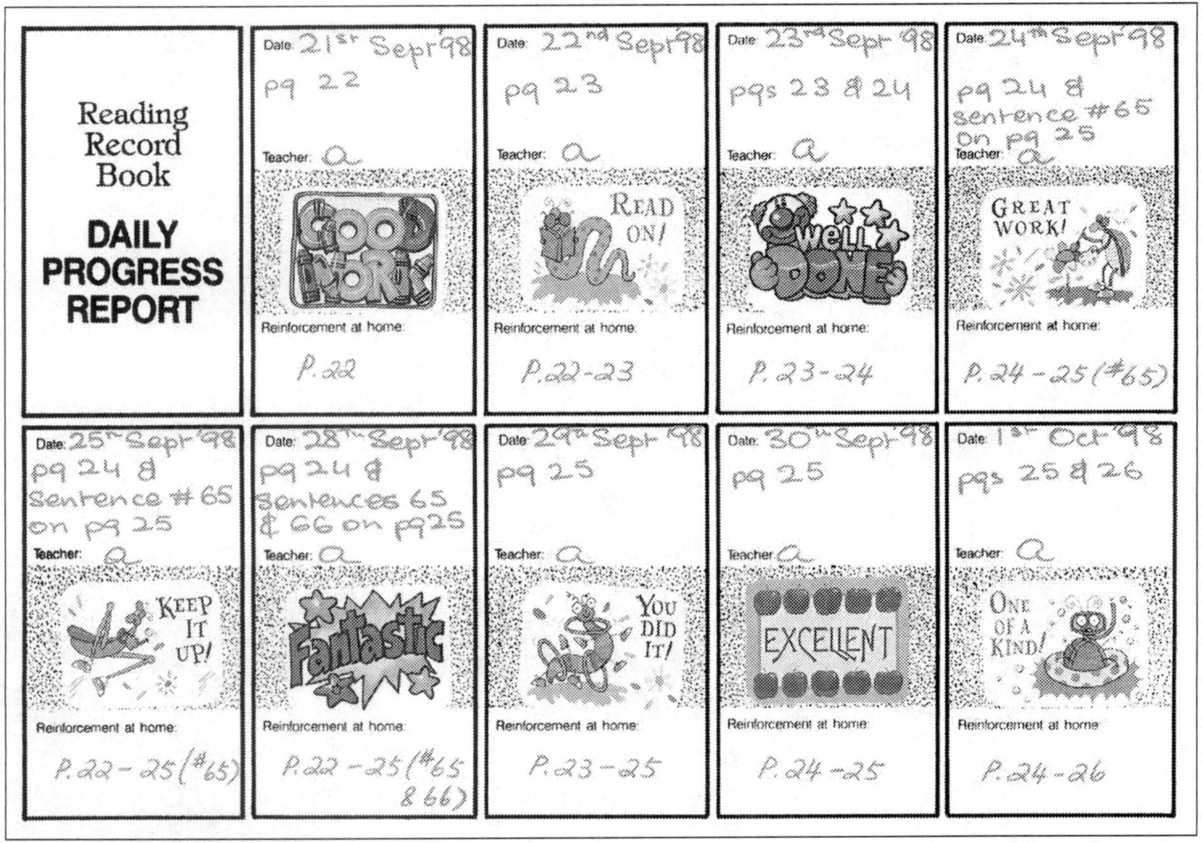
Reading Record Book
DAILY PROGRESS REPORT
Date: 21st Sept 98
pg 22
Teacher: a
GOOD WORK
Reinforcement at home:
P.22
Date: 22nd Sept 98
pg 23
Teacher: a
READ ON!
Reinforcement at home:
P.22-23
Date: 23rd Sept 98
pgs 23 & 24
Teacher: a
WELL DONE
Reinforcement at home:
P.23-24
Date: 24th Sept 98
pg 24 & sentence #65 on pg 25
Teacher: a
GREAT WORK!
Reinforcement at home:
P.24-25(#65)
Date: 25th Sept 98
pg 24 & sentence #65 on pg 25
Teacher: a
KEEP IT UP!
Reinforcement at home:
P.22-25(#65)
Date: 28th Sept 98
pg 24 & sentences 65 & 66 on pg25
Teacher: a
Fantastic
Reinforcement at home:
P.22-25(#65 & 66)
Date: 29th Sept 98
pg 25
Teacher: a
YOU DID IT!
Reinforcement at home:
P.23-25
Date: 30th Sept 98
pg 25
Teacher: a
EXCELLENT
Reinforcement at home:
P.24-25
Date: 1st Oct 98
pgs 25 & 26
Teacher: a
ONE OF A KIND!
Reinforcement at home:
P.24-26

Figure 16: A page from a Reading Record Book

designated child will probably remember his or her assigned role, and so will you, of course, from your list.

Hold up, one at a time, large versions of the words now learned: **UP**, **PUP**, **CUP**, and **CAP**, and for each word, name one of the famous people on your list. "Please read this for us, Santa Claus." The selected child stands, sounds the letters, and reads the word. All applaud. "Read this one, please, Woody Woodpecker." The appropriate child stands, sounds the letters, and reads the word. All applaud.

The entertainment value of the game can be increased if a child can give his performance in a manner suggestive of the person he represents. For example, chosen to read **UP**, Santa Claus might embellish his reading thus: "Ho-ho-ho, *Uh*, *Puh*, up," and Woody Woodpecker might read **CAP**, "Ha-ha-ha-HA-ha, ha-ha-ha-HA-ha, *Cuh*, *A*, *Puh*, cap." Another amusing twist might be introduced by selecting boys to portray female celebrities and girls to portray males.

Day 11: Step 8

The letter today is **T**, pronounced in the special way described on page 44. Perhaps the theme today could be *Tyrannosaurus rex*. Children might come to the front, pinch the corners of their eyes and mouth together, bare their fangs, and say *Tuh* a specified number of times (who's to say *T. rex* didn't actually sound like this?). Or the children themselves might be able to suggest zanier ideas they prefer.

Days 12 and 13: Step 9

On day 12 introduce **AT**, **PAT**, **CAT**, **TAP**, and **CUT** and play the left-to-right game on the chalkboard. On day 13, play the game again, this time adding **UP**, **PUP**, **CUP**, and **CAP**.

Reading to your class

Read to your class at least once a day. You may be the only person some of your pupils ever see reading. When children see how your words project images onto the screen of their minds, they will begin to realize that they have the equivalent of a TV set in their head, and that they can switch it on just by learning to read. You might choose some thick book and read a page or two at each reading session.

A charge commonly leveled at those who teach preschoolers to read is, "Sure, they can read. But do they understand what they're reading?" (This is dealt with in chapter 1.) Such skepticism would be as legitimately voiced for older children who are being read to. Do they understand the words you are reading to them? For example, a story concerning the adventures of a lynx that has a den in the forest is fine, but do the listening children know what a lynx is? a den? a forest? If not, the story will project only blurred images in the children's imaginations, and the story won't be as interesting.

The point is this: vocabulary growth *must* be a part of your reading aloud sessions, just as an explanation of words is essential when teaching preschoolers to read. But instead of stopping your story to explain each novel word that crops up in the text, scan the material beforehand and explain what a lynx is, a den, and a forest. You might even draw a rough representation on the board if pictures aren't handy. (And though you may not regard yourself as being much of an artist, in the children's eyes your manipulation of the chalk will seem magical, and their imaginations will fill in whatever details your drawings lack.)

If you have children in your class who can already read, let them sometimes read aloud to the others. In this way, the other children will see more clearly the goal you want them to reach. They will see, too, that the skill is well within the ability of youngsters their age. A reading child might also read aloud briefly from a comic book; the prospect of eventually reading these colorful next-best-thing-to-TV books is likely to provide an even greater inducement to read than other reading material.

Day 14: Step 10

We introduce **the** today. Have children say the *two* distinct sounds in the word — consonant blend and vowel — while running a finger beneath it (as described in chapter 2, step 10). When all members of the class can perform the ritual accurately, distribute sheets for the stand-up, paper-turning, sit-down game.

The stand-up, paper-turning, sit-down game

Using a sans serif font, print each of the following words in capital letters, and in duplicate, about twelve millimeters (half inch) high: **UP, PUP, CUP, CAP, AT, PAT, CAT, TAP, CUT,** and **the** (see figure 17). Separate the words with scissors and glue them to a sheet of typing paper in a scrambled manner, as shown in figure 17. Photocopy your paste-up and give each child a sheet.

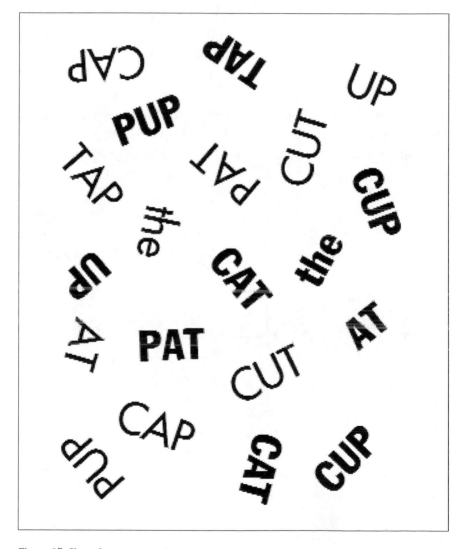

Figure 17: Sheet for paper-turning

To play the game, sound the letters in one of the words, then say the word. Children then jump up and twist the paper to find the word (which is printed *twice* somewhere on the sheet). Pupils are to place a finger on each version of the word, and then sit down. Compliment the speedier players and make a note of those pupils who are going to need extra attention.

An added feature of presenting reading material on paper instead of on the chalkboard is that children then have something to take home. You will thus not only keep parents informed of your teaching efforts and progress, but also give children the opportunity to show their parents how the game is played, and, in the process, gain still more practice with the material. You might include with the sheet a suggestion to parents that they affix the sheet to the refrigerator or the wall so their child can play the game occasionally, perhaps while the parent — busy preparing supper — calls out words. The fact that some of the words will appear upside down to the child will add to the fun. (Nothing lost here. Beginning readers often read words upside down as easily as right side up.)

Posted prominently, the sheets might catch the attention of visitors and prompt further practice: "Benton's been at school less than three weeks, and he's reading already. Terrific teacher. Read for Aunt Ruby, Benton."

Day 15: Step 11
Introduce **H** and lead the class in making the sound correctly, then use any of the methods already described to fix this sound in their minds.

Day 16: Step 12
By referring to the teaching schedule on page 111, you will see that this is the day to introduce **HAT**. Work with **HAT** singly, then add it to the others and play whatever game you wish. Perhaps, in preparation for the lesson, you could show the children how to make paper hats. They could then wear them throughout the reading lesson.

And so on . . .
Having now covered a variety of teaching methods and attention-

getting tactics, little more need be said about day-to-day procedures. The continuing order of presentation is shown in the schedule on pages 110 to 112. As more words are learned, new opportunities arise for prompting repetition.

Here is one final game that you can use when you have introduced the words **HOT**, **HOP**, **TOP**, **POP**, **POT**, **COT**, and **COP** in step 14.

Reading bingo

After completing step 14, your children will be able to read eighteen words. Draw a bingo grid containing sixteen squares. Print sixteen words in the sixteen squares — every word the children can now read except **UP** and **PUP** (which the children should need no further practice with). Photocopy your paste-up and distribute the sheets.

This isn't much of a bingo game because all the sheets are the same and everyone will win at the same time (not that the children need know this). The important thing is that the eyes of every child in the class will be skimming and scanning words in the grid every time you call out a word, and this yields you maximum teaching efficiency. Because you control the order in which words are called out, you will be able to prolong the game as long as possible before a winner (actually, the entire class) shouts a riotous, "Bingo!"

As new sounds and words are learned, you can create bingo grids with more squares, gradually eliminating those words children have no difficulty with, and retaining those that are posing a problem. Of course, if you have time, you can create two or three different bingo cards so that only some of your class emerge as winners.

At this point, your pupils may (or may not) begin to see that, quite aside from the games and the silliness of it all, they are acquiring the ability to pry open the contents of words — much in the way one might discover the contents of unlabeled tinned foods by using a can-opener. As this new skill takes shape in their minds, so the need for games will diminish. For you, however, the games will continue to serve an important function by letting you gear your progress to the slowest children, and do so without boring the quicker children.

Be sure to periodically send home lists for display around the children's homes containing all the words your pupils can now read.

Include, of course, the usual request that parents exhibit the material prominently, so friends, neighbors, and relatives can compliment their youngster on his or her advancing reading ability.

On or about day 43, your class will be ready to begin reading the first two hundred sentences, dealt with in chapter 8.

SUGGESTED READING

When you can teach a class of children to read with complete success in one school year, you have little need for textbooks to support your views on reading technology or on teaching methods. Success requires neither defence nor elaboration. *You* are the expert — you have no need to read the following books except that reading technology is an interesting subject, and you, as a practising expert, might find this branch of learning fascinating. Here are a few works I have found to be both interesting and important, and which I think can add greatly to your stature as an all-round reading authority.

Mitford Mathews *Teaching to Read, Historically Considered* (University of Chicago Press, 1966).

This entertaining book reveals some of the monumental, often comical blunders that have been committed throughout history in the name of teaching children to read, blunders that ultimately led to creation of the faulty whole word approach to reading, still found in classrooms today in the form of whole language.

Rudolf Flesch *Why Johnny Still Can't Read* (Harper and Row, 1981).

This book is a follow-up to Flesch's earlier work, *Why Johnny Can't Read*, which remained on the best-seller list for thirty weeks beginning in 1955 — a bombshell that generated forces for changes in teaching reading, forces that, alas, gradually died, and changes that regrettably never materialized. The book reveals the pitfalls and failings of popular reading programs still in use.

Jeanne Chall *Learning to Read: The Great Debate* (McGraw-Hill, 1983).

This is probably the most frequently cited work in any serious discussion of reading technology. Dr. Chall is generally regarded as the pre-eminent researcher of reading programs. Under a grant from the Carnegie Foundation, Dr. Chall visited more than three hundred classrooms (kindergarten and grades 1, 2, and 3) in the U.S., England, and Scotland to see what worked and what didn't work in reading instruction.

William J. Bennett *The De-Valuing of America* (Summit Books, 1992).

The chapter entitled "Crisis in American Education" provides a startling revelation of the powerful forces working quietly against improvements in public schooling, told by the most inside of insiders: a former U.S. secretary of education.

Samuel L. Blumenfeld *The Whole Language/OBE Fraud* (The Paradigm Company, 1996).

An encyclopedic account of the curiously errant twists of thought that have sundered reading instruction in North America over the past 150 years, culminating in the dumbing-down practices now used that perpetuate illiteracy and enfeeble children's spelling and math ability.

7

Teaching Your
Schoolchild

This chapter has two parts. The first, "Teaching an untaught school-age child," deals with teaching a youngster who has started school but has received little or no reading instruction. This would normally be junior- and senior-kindergartners, and grade 1 pupils during their first month or two in school. However, if your child has received more than two months of reading instruction, and guesses at words, pursue the program in the second part of the chapter, "Correcting a school-child's faulty reading."

We will employ many of the same procedures that were used for preschoolers in chapter 3, but altered to suit your older child. If you haven't read chapter 3 yet, read it now so you may clearly understand the comments and instructions that follow.

The main difference between teaching a preschooler and a school-age child is that the older child is usually better able to deal with abstractions, has a longer attention span, and is more likely to understand and appreciate the value of reading. For these reasons he or she is likely to be easier to teach.

But this is a generalization. Maturity can also bring special problems for older children if they have already decided — from observing those around them — that conversation, TV, and video games adequately fill their informational and entertainment needs. Such children may be less enthusiastic about tackling a communications system that seems to require a lot of work. Yet, just as three-year-old Marcia was enticed to pursue the reading program in chapter 3, so an older child can be humored along the path to literacy. On the other hand, if fate should favor you with a school-age child who is enthusiastic about learning to read, your task is simple.

PLANNING YOUR PROGRAM

As explained for the instruction of preschoolers in chapter 3, you will need to decide on a schedule for teaching your school-age child. How long you devote to the program each day will depend on his or her attention span and enthusiasm, as well as on what other after-school activities you both have.

As was suggested for the instruction of a preschooler, you may want to consider engaging a young tutor to take on some or all of the reading instruction. School-age children will often cooperate more readily with someone outside the family. Moreover, such an arrangement frees you to deal with other matters. See the comments starting on page 80 for engaging a young teaching assistant. Take care, though, about hiring someone too close in age to your child; a youngster will have more respect for, and will more willingly follow, the guidance of someone at least a few years older.

WHAT ABOUT YOUR CHILD'S PUBLIC SCHOOL TEACHER?

Parents sometimes wonder what their child's schoolteacher might think about instructing a child at home, so let's address the question.

Kindergarten teachers aren't usually involved with reading instruction. At most, they might introduce children to the alphabet and teach their pupils the *names* of the letters (which, as explained in chapter 1, is what we *don't* want). Grade 1 teachers, though, may or may not be concerned about parents teaching reading at home. But, regardless of what the teacher's thinking and attitude is, your child's guaranteed literacy is our first concern, and it must pre-empt every other consideration.

As a general rule, it is better to wait for the teacher to show interest in your home instruction. Our purpose isn't to compete with class-room instruction, but to supplement it, and because we can't predict the beliefs and attitude of your child's teacher, the safest plan is for you to proceed with your home instruction program without drawing attention to it. The ratio of one child to one teacher (the teacher being you) favors quicker and surer success than does the classroom ratio of thirty pupils to one schoolteacher, especially as the grade 1 teacher may be burdened in other ways — possibly even with a hum-drum and faulty reading program.

Additionally, parents would be wise to avoid any criticism of a schoolteacher's performance in their child's presence. Pursue your program quietly. Don't make waves. If your child surges ahead of the others and the teacher thinks it's because of her good teaching, why prick the bubble? Your child's superb reading may alleviate a few of the teacher's other headaches better than a handful of aspirin. If you wish, you can always inform the teacher at the end of the school year of your involvement (if, in fact, he or she hasn't already guessed it).

In short, don't push for a meeting or a collaborative arrangement with your child's teacher. If the teacher wants to discuss your program with you, he or she will let you know. But remember, your child and his or her reading progress constitute only one-thirtieth of the teacher's concerns.

TO WORK

The activities described in chapter 3 for teaching a preschooler will, in general, work equally well for an older child. However, you will know best whether the use of puppets is appropriate. The value of the teaching machine (the blocks game) for ensuring rapid advancement remains the same for the older child, though you may have to use different rewards. And payment may have to be made differently too: whereas a three-year-old requires immediate gratification, an older child may work diligently for some delayed reward. A penny or two placed in each cup might be adequate enticement, if the child sees that pennies will eventually permit the purchase of some desired item costing several dollars.

Much of the glitz and hoopla suggested for use with a three-year-old may be unnecessary with your older child. Will your child be captivated by the antics of stuffed animals? Would he or she enjoy having a special area of a room assigned to serve as school? These are matters for you to decide. Your preparations may require only the construction of the blocks game. Whether you conduct your program at a table or on the floor is another matter best decided by you. Pick a time of day or evening for your reading lessons that doesn't conflict with some other pleasurable activity your child would normally engage in.

Finally, you may be surprised how quickly your child learns to read, and you may feel, in consequence, a constant tug to proceed ever more quickly. Resist the urge. Be wary of advancing too speedily. Never, *ever*, underestimate the value of review.

TEACHING AN UNTAUGHT SCHOOL-AGE CHILD

For a clearer picture of the challenges to be faced in teaching an untaught school-age child, and some ways of dealing with them, we might look over the shoulders of parents engaging in the procedure. Let's draft a brief scenario for Rebecca, age five, whose parents, Ken Hoffman and Nancy Klein, think it would be a good idea if their daughter got started reading before grade 1. They agree to split the duties. Nancy will do the teaching and Ken will construct the blocks game, prepare the printed materials, and cheer Rebecca's every advance.

Their program is soon in operation. On arriving home with Rebecca from the daycare center (where Rebecca is bused from kindergarten),

Nancy teaches for a few minutes before preparing supper. Everything goes well, and when Daddy arrives home, Rebecca proudly reads the word **UP** for him. Greatly impressed, Daddy, with simple sleight of hand and subtle misdirection, seems to pluck a twenty-five-cent piece out of Rebecca's ear. He discloses that the "ear money" — which will appear each day — can be saved to buy Barbie doll clothes — of special interest to Rebecca.

Intrigued by his daughter's quick advancement, yet feeling left out of things, Ken asks Nancy if, while she works on supper, he might play the blocks game with Rebecca. Fine, so long as he merely reviews the word **UP**. He doesn't listen, of course, and soon introduces the word **PUP** to the game. Nancy catches him before he introduces the letter **C**, so, while the dumplings simmer, he is obliged to turn to the office work he brought home.

With two reading sessions each day, one with Nancy and one with Ken, and double sessions on the weekend, Rebecca has almost enough money at the end of the first week to outfit Barbie with a wedding dress, and can read **UP**, **PUP**, **CUP**, and **CAP**.

Hearing of Rebecca's quick reading progress, neighbors Ernie and Helen Topaz think the reading program might be ideal for their son Kevin, age six, who has been in grade 1 for four months and can now identify several words that form sentences in a school reader. But Kevin's "reading" is more of a recitation. He can read only the words in the school book, and none other — in or out of books. Kevin hasn't been taught the sounds of the letters, or if he has, he hasn't been exercised in using them, nor shown how to use that information to learn the identity of words he hasn't memorized.

The Topazes think Kevin would progress more quickly if they supplemented his school instruction with phonic instruction at home. So, armed with this book, Ernie promptly constructs the blocks game and prints the required materials. He and his wife have decided they will leave Kevin's instruction wholly to Anne, their fifteen-year-old baby-sitter, who will teach Kevin on the two nights a week when the Topazes are out.

What rewards will go into the cups of the blocks game? Kevin has been agitating for a basketball net to be installed beside the driveway.

His father had planned to buy one, but now Ernie thinks, *How much better if Kevin were to earn the basketball net. He would then appreciate the device all the more, and take satisfaction in having earned it. Good for self-reliance and self-esteem.*

Accordingly, Ernie supplies Anne with a stock of poker chips to place in the egg cups. Each chip is to represent five cents toward Kevin's eighty-five-dollar basketball stand and net. Helen has already gone over the first letter sounds with Anne and shows her the relevant pages in the book in case she needs more information.

Kevin gets a goodnight kiss and a final farewell as his parents leave. The farewell falls on deaf ears: Kevin is already engrossed in the blocks game — a yellow brick road that will lead to a basketball net — and before his parents' car leaves the driveway he has mastered **U** and **P** and is reading his first word, **UP**. Ring up sixty cents.

Kevin vetoes Anne's every attempt to stop the game. By the time his parents reach the theater, Kevin has mastered the sounds **C** and **A**, and is now reading **UP**, **PUP**, **CUP**, and **CAP**, with a great amount of review achieved by four more trips along the base of the blocks game. Ring up another $2.40.

When Mr. and Mrs. Topaz arrive home that night, they are surprised to see the light still on in Kevin's room. Thank heavens the child is in bed — as he should be. But he's still playing the blocks game with Anne, and has rung up a total of $18.60. Kevin grins. Anne apologizes. The parents exchange glances.

The next day, for his parent's satisfaction, Kevin goes through the list of words he can now sound out and read, and ends by wondering whether his parents might go out more often than twice a week.

Ken Hoffman chats up Ernie Topaz about the idea of a pen pal arrangement between Kevin and Rebecca — not real messages, of course, just an exchange of printed words each child can read. The fathers are soon stuffing their children's printed words into envelopes and delivering them, and Kevin and Rebecca take great pride in the fact they are sending letters to each other, just as adults do. So, still another motivating force begins contributing to the children's reading enjoyment: a force generated solely by pride of accomplishment.

Children will often participate in a complicated procedure solely for the reward of parental attention. Others will need enticements to pursue an activity that yields no other immediately discernible benefit. Justification for initial use of extrinsic rewards was dealt with in chapter 2. However, when children begin to see how the connection of letters and letter sounds, and the synthesis of these sounds, project recognizable images onto the screen of the mind, the need for external rewards diminishes. Until that time, though, we are wise to entice youngsters along avenues that we know will eventually blossom into vistas of reading delight.

Rebecca and Kevin now read skilfully. Barbie has the necessary nuptial garment (plus a complete honeymoon wardrobe), and the Topazes' driveway has become the most popular one on the block.

CORRECTING A SCHOOLCHILD'S FAULTY READING

No failing in modern education receives more attention from the media than reading failure. And with good reason: when children lack the ability to read well, their academic future is severely restricted, and when they achieve adulthood their social standing and professional achievement is invariably impoverished.

Standard instructional methods in grade 1 initiate reading problems. Weak grade 2 instruction helps to perpetuate the problems. But a more subtle and long-lasting harm is inflicted by educational authorities who, in presuming to find a cause for children's reading problems, place the burden of failure on children and their families. Experts probe the children's manners, habits, and home-life, wholly ignoring the type of instruction the children have received. Teaching methods are never questioned, nor even regarded as suspect. Children and their environments are seen as the sole cause of reading failure.

Presumed authorities sometimes cloud matters with self-serving logic. For example, one supposed expert (a pediatrician who heads a reading disability clinic in San Diego) says the smart thing to do is simply accept the fact that some children aren't cut out for reading, and steer them into vocations that don't require literacy (which might prompt one to think that some pediatricians aren't cut out for theorizing about educational matters). Other authorities contend that at least ten percent of children are afflicted with dyslexia. Newspapers seize on these absurdities, which are then welcomed by all those in education who can't teach reading effectively.

I personally contend that dyslexia is, with few exceptions, the product of faulty reading programs: a matter dealt with at length in the appendix to this book.

Agreed, some children have sufficient emotional difficulties to greatly impede progress at school (though we have never encountered such a child at our reading clinic). The problem suffered by the youngsters we see aren't familial but tutorial. They simply haven't been told certain basic and necessary details. And lacking this essential information, they easily form a distorted picture of their ability to learn. Children who entered school self-assured and brimming with confidence begin to question their ability. What should such children think? Are they dummies, or do they lack some special aptitude for reading?

In most cases, the only thing the failing children lack is the ability to puzzle out, on their own, the letter sounds that may or may not have even been taught to them. The fact that their classmates were able to sort out — with varying degrees of success (and perhaps with some help from home) — the connection between letters and letter sounds isn't reason to think there is anything wrong with children who can't do the same. Everyone — adults and children alike — regardless of intelligence, has strengths and weaknesses in deductive reasoning ability.

And so, children who entered school with no afflictions now have one, but it's one much more devastating than a mere reading difficulty. They suffer a loss of self-esteem.

What is so special about self-esteem? The California Task Force to Promote Self-Esteem and Personal and Social Responsibility responds:

Self-esteem is the likeliest candidate for a "social vaccine," something that empowers us to live responsibly and that inoculates us against the lure of crime, violence, substance abuse . . . and educational failure.

Other long-term failings can erupt, surprisingly enough, from a primary teacher's low estimation of a failing pupil. Dr. Eigil Pedersen, professor of education at McGill University, discovered a vast difference in adult performance that was linked with the attitude of grade 1 teachers. One group in the study had benefited from the positive influence of a grade 1 teacher who had encouraged children's self-esteem. A second group had suffered the negative influence of a grade 1 teacher who had generated in children doubts about their abilities.

As adults, the conduct and abilities of the two groups were consistent with what the grade 1 teachers had *thought* about the children's abilities. The children's early beliefs — based on their grade 1 teacher's opinion — had become self-fulfilling prophecies, ones that had influenced not only their way of life, but, more surprisingly, their adult IQ ratings.*

Regrettably, then, the opinion formed of stumbling readers by a mistaken grade 1 teacher can diminish children's self-esteem and lower their performance not only in school, but also later, in adult life.

Once children accept the notion that they have a special difficulty in reading — or worse, that they have a special difficulty in learning or even in thinking — and develop a self-image of incompetency, they can become virtually hypnotized by that notion.

Alerted to the avenues of danger that branch from faulty instruction, you will better appreciate the need for immediate remedy, a remedy you are now well equipped to provide. Let's look at the usual causes of faulty reading.

The schoolchildren we see at our reading clinic suffer from one or both of the following failings.

1. They have been inadequately taught the letter sounds, or, if taught the sounds, they haven't been shown, or practised in, the use of the sounds as a means of determining what a word is.
2. They have spent little time reading, either in school or at home,

---

* E. Pedersen and T. Faucher, with W. W. Eaton, "A New Perspective on the Effects of First-Grade Teachers on Children's Subsequent Adult Status," *Harvard Educational Review* (1978): 1–31.

and their parents have failed to monitor their child's reading progress.

This last pronouncement might seem to lay blame on parents for not keeping tabs on their child's reading ability, but most parents hold the view that reading instruction is the professionals' business. Furthermore, they may have been lulled into an acceptance of faulty reading performance with the bromide, "Don't worry if your child doesn't read this year; he'll read when he's ready." Such parents watch as their non-reading child advances to grade 2, then, still barely reading, moves on to grade 3. All the while, their child's report card gives no hint that there is anything to worry about. Then the experts — usually prodded into motion by concerned parents — are stirred to search and identify what they consider to be wrong with the child. And they are skilful at finding failings in children and their home environments.

But let's put aside the various possible causes of your child's reading problem, and concentrate on solving that problem.

The most common complaints made of a schoolchild's reading are (1) the child doesn't read well and often guesses at words, or (2) the child can read, but doesn't properly understand what he or she has read, or (3) the child can read, but rarely does. All three complaints may be the result of the same cause.

To illustrate: a child who has an insecure knowledge and use of the letter-sound code will naturally read with greater difficulty than a child who has been expertly taught the sounds (complaint 1). And if, because of poor reading ability, a child reads sentences too slowly to scoop its contents together into a clear picture of the writer's intent, the child won't fully understand what he reads (complaint 2). And because children's reading abilities vary, some children passing as readers may still find reading too burdensome to be enjoyable (complaint 3). In truth, children who can read skilfully and have easy access to books on subjects they find fascinating, won't have to reminded or prodded to read.

When parents begin to suspect their child has a reading problem (despite good marks or favorable comments from school), they sometimes arrange a meeting with the school principal. The following scenario is pretty much in keeping with the reports we receive from parents who bring their children to our remedial reading clinic.

A meeting with the principal

The parents — let's call them the O'Reillys — notice their nine-year-old son, Woodrow, in grade 3, still can't read. In the past, they have been apprehensive. Now they're worried.

The principal, Mr. Cook, is sympathetic and completely understanding of their concern. He explains fatalistically that children learn to read at different speeds; that some children learn to read much later than others; and that he is confident the day will come when Woodrow's reading will spurt ahead and nothing will be able to hold him back.

Nodding, but not wholly convinced, the O'Reillys wonder if there could be anything wrong with the teaching or the reading program. Mr. Cook points out that if this were the case, the other children wouldn't be reading so well. The O'Reillys thank Mr. Cook for his time and leave, hoping the principal's prophesy comes true.

Regrettably, school principals are usually as much in the dark as parents on a key matter concerning reading skill. What isn't generally known is that publishers of reading books commonly issue their writers lists of words they must limit themselves to when writing their stories. In this way the tightly controlled vocabularies used in the books will match the limited number of words children are taught to memorize in the word-memorization method of instruction promoted by the publisher's reading program.

Two failings of such programs are, first, that not all children are able to memorize the required number of words; and second, that children who are able to memorize the words are often unable to read words other than those they have memorized.

Where does *your* child's problem really lie?

To identify the root of your child's reading problem, have him or her read the following words and sentences:

cuff zip frost

blink plump bud

RON FED HIS PET RAT A YAM

JAN SAW A TIN OF WAX IN THE HUT *

Into which of the following categories does your child fit?

Child A: can't read the words accurately, and guesses.

Child B: can read the words with some accuracy but not quickly. The speed and correctness with which your child reads the test material will give you a good idea how well he or she has been taught the phonic letter-code, or how well exercised the child has been in using that information.

Child C: reads the text easily, but as a rule doesn't read very often.

The bulk of this chapter is written for Child A and Child B. Getting Child C to read more often is dealt with in the last few pages of part 4.

The challenges

There are three separate challenges in overcoming a reading problem. The first challenge lies in convincing your child that he or she isn't to blame for reading poorly, but that the fault lies with the poor reading program his or her teacher had to use, and if the teacher had been given the reading program you now have, your child wouldn't have a reading problem.

The second challenge lies in securing your child's cooperation: a task that may be difficult or not, depending on his or her attitude and degree of interest in being able to read skilfully, and the level of success you usually have in securing the youngster's cooperation in any venture. The worst-case scenario would be an uncooperative child who

---

* Devised by Dr. Mary Johnson, author of *Programmed Illiteracy in Our Schools*; Dr. Ruth Weir, school trustee and former junior grade teacher for twenty years, and author of *The Literate Elite*; and this author.

has no desire to improve his or her faulty reading (a venomous situation for which we have a powerful antidote).

In addition to securing your child's cooperation, we will need to counteract the defeatist attitude he or she may have developed toward reading, for such could frustrate even the best instruction — a matter illuminatingly reported in the book, *Self-Consistency*, by Prescott Lecky.

Dr. Lecky found that students tended to perform poorly in subjects in which success would be inconsistent with the image they held of themselves. Dr. Lecky cites cases showing that when one's conception of self (or perhaps better, self-deception) is suitably altered, and the individual is made to realize that success in a particular subject need not stir inner conflict, success invariably follows.

Such a change in the pupil's attitude often results in improvement which is quite astonishing. A high school student who misspelled 55 words out of a hundred, and who failed so many subjects that he lost credit for a full year, became one of the best spellers in the school during the next year, and made a general average of 91. A student who was dropped from another college and was later admitted to Columbia was graduated with more than 70 points of "A" credits. A boy failing in English, who had been diagnosed by a testing bureau as lacking aptitude for his subject, won honorable mention a year later for the literary prize at a large preparatory school. A girl who had failed four times in Latin, with marks between 20 and 50, after three talks with the school counsellor made a mark of 92 on the next test and finished with a grade of 84. She is now taking advanced Latin with grades above 80.*

Your child is nowhere near this elevated level of education; however, the more we know of the bizarre forces that work at all levels to speed or slow learning, the better we can address them, and by doing so, advance your child more easily and quickly.

The third challenge faced in advancing your child's reading ability lies in discouraging well-established faulty reading habits and replacing them with good habits. What sort of habits?

---

* Prescott Lecky, *Self-Consistency* (Shoe String Press, 1961).

The clearest and most distinctive evidence of poor reading instruction is a child's constant resort to guessing when trying to read. So first we must stop your pupil from guessing. This restriction will not be popularly received, for you are asking him or her to alter the habit of an academic lifetime — a habit that has become second nature to the youngster.

CREATING A REMEDIAL READING PROGRAM

Begin by studying chapter 2. Learn to make the letter sounds correctly. Then read chapter 3, "Teaching Your Preschooler," which describes techniques that will be equally useful in teaching your older child. For example, the blocks game — so simple that even a two-year-old can play it — will work no less effectively for your eight-, ten-, twelve-, or fourteen-year-old, so long as you increase the rewards suitably.

There are at least four different ways to proceed with your remedial reading program. The best method for you will be determined by the amount of time you can give to the task, the amount of cooperation you can expect from your child, and how motivated he or she is to become a skilful reader.

Method 1: You as the sole teacher

Let's begin with the most difficult case: an uncooperative child who doesn't want to learn to read. The methods we use in this extreme situation will help you decide what lesser measures are appropriate for your situation.

With such a child, we work a simple exchange: something for something. We want the child to read skilfully. He or she isn't interested. Perhaps there is something the child would like to have — designer clothes, sports equipment, CDs, a video tape, a ticket to an upcoming rock concert or sports event, or a visit to a theme park or amusement center. Whatever the desired item is, there lies the baited hook.

Bribery? Not at all. Just fair compensation for effort given to a task the child finds disagreeable. How is the child's situation different from that of others who engage in disagreeable work for financial reward?

The highly efficient blocks game, described in chapter 3, provides the means by which our reluctant learner can secure the prized item. Let's suppose — and remember this is a worst-case arrangement — let's suppose we had to put as much as a dime in each of the egg cups to capture and hold the child's interest. And let's further suppose that to improve the child's reading to where he or she begins to take pride in this new-found skill, it costs thirty or forty dollars, paid out in a parade of dimes. This seemingly great expense would, in fact, be a bargain. Consider: just a single one-hour session at a professional tutoring center (where your child would probably have to share the teacher with two other children) would cost approximately the same amount.

Most parents will probably try to remedy their child's reading problem themselves before resorting to other ways that will be described later. Let's consider the case of Juliet Martino, sister of Nancy Klein, whose daughter's reading adventure was described in the first part of this chapter.

When Juliet hears of her niece Rebecca's rapid reading advancement, she sees possible salvation for her seven-year-old son, Mario, who has been labeled learning disadvantaged. Now in grade 2, Mario often guesses words when he tries to read them, and he occasionally reads words backwards. However, Mario is the personification of obstinacy, and has always refused Juliet's attempts to help him with his reading (though, admittedly, she wasn't quite sure what his problem was). Now, having studied the first few chapters of this book, Juliet reasons that her son guesses words because he hasn't learned the letter sounds — or at least hasn't learned how the letter sounds can be used to figure out the identity of words he hasn't encountered in print before, and that he sometimes reads words backwards because the left-to-right reading procedure is insecurely fixed in his mind. When Juliet asks Mario to read the test words and sentences on page 143, he makes a half-hearted attempt, but is quickly stumped.

Employing the ingenuity single parents are sometimes obliged to cultivate, Juliet constructs the blocks game and prints the words needed for Mario's reading advancement, all the while knowing that her greatest problem will lie in securing his cooperation.

Her worst fear is quickly realized. Mario balks at participating in the reading game which, to him, is merely an instrument that will reaffirm his stupidity. (He is regarded as the number one dummy in his class.) Juliet shelves the blocks game and printed materials and enters a "deep-think" mode to find a solution.

What would make Mario cooperate in the reading venture? He wants a rabbit. That's out. Rabbit, rabbit cage, rabbit food, rabbit smell — not to mention the droppings. Ugh. And yet, if a rabbit is to be the price of Mario's ascent to literacy, perhaps she should bite the bullet. She'll do it.

That night, chatting up the possibility that they *might* get a rabbit, Juliet spells out the terms of the arrangement. Mario must promise to take care of the feeding, watering, exercising, and, uh, you know what. Juliet will buy the rabbit and the whole kit and caboodle, as soon as they complete chapter 3 of the book. Is he interested? You bet!

The blocks game is immediately put to use. Mario sees no big deal in learning the sound of **U** and **P** and putting them together to read **UP**, and he begins to wonder why he was reluctant to engage in so trivial a procedure. Naturally, he can't see the importance of the simple routines he is so primitively employing: assigning the correct sounds to letters, and sounding out those letters from left to right, never from right to left.

Mario's enthusiasm for the reading game grows daily when he finds each step so simple he can't fail. A weight seems to be removed from his shoulders when he sees he doesn't come off looking dumb. Soon, his obstinacy takes the more profitable form of refusing to end each reading session when Juliet requests it — which, of course, secretly delights her — as he begins to take pride in his rapidly advancing reading skill.

Method 2: Parent-team instruction

If you lack the confidence to handle the remedial program alone, find another child who is also having difficulty with the letter code. You and that child's parent could collaborate by taking turns teaching both children at your respective homes. A joint venture of this sort will strengthen both parents' confidence, and the presence of a second child will make reading instruction more enjoyable for each.

If you don't know anyone whose child has a reading problem, have your child get the phone numbers of classmates who are reading poorly. Phone the parents. Chat them up; get their feelings about their child's poor reading. Would they be interested in working with you in a shared remedial reading plan? If so, meet and explain the program and work out a combined strategy. An ice-cream-and-cookies celebration after each reading session would probably increase the children's interest.

The following example offers a few useful ideas.

When Mrs. Jay's eleven-year-old piano pupil, Joan, arrives for her lesson, the youngster proudly announces she has learned to play a new piece, "Minuet," all by herself. One problem: the title of the piece — in one-inch-high letters at the top of the music — is "Mimic." Asked to sound out the letters in the word, Joan can't get any closer than "Mimsey."

Puzzled, and now suspicious about her own nine-year-old son's reading ability, Mrs. Jay tests him and finds to her distress that Grant can't read the simple word *mop* because, as he explains, "We haven't taken it."*

When she tests Kingsley Offenbach, a neighbor's child — also in grade three — Mrs. Jay finds she isn't the only parent with a problem. The Jays and the Offenbachs confer and decide that, though they could storm the school, their energies would be better spent teaching their children to read. Finding this book, they study chapters 2 and 3 in preparation for the venture, and work out a collaborative program to be conducted on alternate nights in each other's homes.

Employing inventiveness, the two families devise a system that will motivate the boys to teach themselves with minimal adult guidance. First, the rewards. Kingsley wants a ping-pong table, and Grant, a remote-controlled model airplane kit. Done! Each child is guaranteed his reward when he can read — skilfully and without guessing — the first hundred words as presented in chapter 2. The boys will receive

---

*   This incident, a cut-and-paste tribute to a Canadian pioneer and champion for reading reform, Dr. Mary Johnson, is completely true and eventually led her to write the book *Programmed Illiteracy in Our Schools* (Clarity Books, 1970).

initial instruction and, as they progress, will be given more information and be shown how to use that information in the blocks game. The youngsters are to cut the slips for attachment to the blocks, print the letters and words on the slips, and finally, play the blocks game without bothering anyone.

The parents puzzle out a twist for the blocks game that eliminates the need for a reward in every cup. The first eleven cups of the blocks game will be empty and the twelfth will contain several jellybeans. In the normal playing of the blocks game, players can easily predict, by counting alternate moves, who will end up landing opposite the last cup. In this version of the game, the boys are to flip a coin each time to determine who will take the next turn. This means that one youngster might have two or three turns in a row. But the luckiest turn is the one that lands the player beside the jellybeans.

The boys are told they can play the game for as long as they choose. When they want more letter sound information to include in the game, they are to call a parent.

It is hardly surprising that the boys, energized — nay, propelled — by visions of a ping-pong table and a remote-controlled model airplane, speed along the base of the blocks game many times every evening from Monday to Friday, calling out periodically for more letter sound information to include in their game. By Friday night, Grant and Kingsley can read without fault twenty-five words (to the end of step 16), which they have increased to twenty-six words by cleverly including the word *a* (a word not listed as part of the program). With the scent of ping-pong balls and model-airplane fuel heavy in their nostrils, the boys perform a sort of Grand Prix reading effort on Saturday and Sunday, and by Sunday night, with an additional thirty words learned (to the end of step 23), they oblige their parents to realize that the day of financial reckoning is fast approaching.

The boys soon have their respective rewards. But then, ah-h-h, there's the matter of a precision fuel-injection device and manifold-centrifugal-alignment kit, special batteries for the remote-control unit, plus a custom-designed container to serve as both hangar and protective unit for transporting the plane to and from its place of flight.

Then, ahem, there's the matter of high-priced ping-pong bats (auto-graphed by the reigning Icelandic champion) featuring molded professional grips, and designer high-traction ping-pong footwear (also autographed by the reigning Icelandic champion). So it's back to the blocks game as the boys proceed with the first 200 sentences, described in chapter 8.

Two months have now passed. The ping-pong table, the model airplane, and the various appurtenances have all been secured. So has Grant and Kingsley's literacy.

Method 3: Instruction by personal tutor

As stated in chapter 4, babysitters are a good potential source of excellent private tutors. Your child may cooperate more readily, and enjoy the learning procedure more, when it is conducted by an older child; the approval and compliments of an older child are often treasured more than those of an adult. You merely need teach the tutor a specific letter sound before each lesson and explain what procedure to follow. This will leave you free to attend to other matters around the home.

Method 4: Your child as teacher

In this arrangement, your child would teach a non-reader to read: a procedure that lets him or her save face (if that is a problem) and gain the satisfaction of teaching another to read.

You need only find a parent who would like to have her preschooler taught to read. This done, teach your child before each lesson only the material he or she needs to know for that particular teaching session. By teaching another child, your youngster will learn, and gain experience in using, the reading procedures he or she lacks.

You could work out an arrangement of payment or reward (which might appear to come from the parent of the preschooler, but actually be paid by you) for your child's tutoring service. As the younger pupil's reading advances, so will your child's.

Perhaps other teaching arrangements are coming to your mind, ones better suited to your situation. Pursue whatever system you find most attractive.

When your child eventually completes the Helpful Andrew stories (part 4), then what? *Tempt* your child to read in as many ways as you can think of. A number of techniques are presented, beginning on page 210, in part 4. Choose those you feel are best suited to your situation.

THE FIRST 200 SENTENCES AND BEYOND

Introduction to Part Three

Your learner is now well launched on our reading adventure, having passed through a low cloud-cover of words, soon to pass through the brighter realm of sentences, and then, at escape velocity, to travel out into the orbit of books.

In chapter 8 we first construct simple sentences with the words your child or pupil can already read, then gradually introduce those letters not yet dealt with: *F, L, M, J, W, V, X, Z, QU, Y,* and *K.* Finally, we will consider some common letter combinations that create their own special sounds — *er, or, sh, ch,* and so on.

The most difficult part of your child's journey from illiteracy to literacy is already behind you. From now on, the job becomes easier because the content of sentences provides, in itself, an interesting reward for your pupil's cooperation and effort — a reward made all the more entertaining by *silly sentence reviews,* which you will soon learn about. Once your child sees how a series of printed words can create interesting comments, questions, and even humor, he or she will become even more enthusiastic about reading. If you are ready for a few surprises and perhaps a few laughs, let's proceed with chapter 8.

8

The First
200 Sentences

The material in this chapter alternates between providing instruction for parents/teachers and introducing sentences that contain new letter sounds. Those teaching a class would, of course, copy some of the material onto a chalkboard.

ABOUT READING SENTENCES

When you read a sentence — as, for example, *this* sentence — you process words so speedily that when you arrive at the end of the sentence, you still remember the opening words and the preparation that was made for what followed — as you have just done. But a beginning reader can't do this, sometimes not even with short sentences. The ability to scoop together a procession of words into an identifiable thought calls for advanced ability. This ability comes only with practice: a point sometimes overlooked by parents of schoolchildren who report that their child "can read all right, but he doesn't understand what he reads." There is usually nothing wrong with the child;

the difficulty lies with his or her poor reading ability. If, by the time the child has labored through to the end of a sentence, he has forgotten how the sentence began, he will naturally have a fuzzy understanding of its message.

The ability to read easily and unhesitatingly is therefore of supreme importance if children are to fully understand what they read. So, don't worry if your learner doesn't immediately catch the thoughts conveyed in some of the sentences presented. Understanding will grow as reading skill advances.

THE 43 STEPS

Step 1: The first sentences
The first fifteen sentences, shown on page 159, are composed mainly from the hundred words your pupil learned to read earlier. The difference now is that the words convey statements and observations. But first, your child must learn that the left-to-right movement used when sounding letters in words prevails similarly for the *series* of words we call sentences. To help your youngster grasp this point, encourage him or her to move a finger from left to right beneath the first word in a sentence, then continue the motion beneath the second, third, and remaining words. You might see a look of surprise — perhaps even an explosion of delight — when the youngster realizes that the three words convey a statement.

Sentences 1 to 4 are straightforward, with nothing new here. Sentence 5 contains a new word, *had*, which your pupil should easily be able to sound out and understand. In sentences 6 and 7, a final *S* has been added to words, a variation your pupil encountered earlier in *cats*, *pots*, and *cups*.

In sentence 7, an apostrophe appears for the first time. There's no need for a major explanation (which might confuse matters). Children usually accept deviations and novelties without the logical explanation an adult might require. Also, in the word *don't*, your pupil encounters for the first time the other sound *O* can represent. Just say, "Here we say *owe* instead of *awe*," and let the child sound out the letters to discover what the word is. Help only if necessary.

In sentence 9, your learner encounters the letter *K* for the first time, introduced here, in an incidental way, along with *C*. In sentences 10 to 15, the letter *S* takes on a new sound — a buzzing sound — in *is* and *has*. Again, offer no explanation other than, "That's the way it is." Don't feel you are personally accountable for every idiosyncrasy of our language.

Perhaps a word is in order on the matter of adaptation. By adaptation, I mean the puzzling-out skill learners develop to interpret letter sounds in a loose exploratory way: a wrinkle that permits them to identify words containing new or misleading letter combinations. To illustrate, I have seen two- and three-year-olds who, having had no instruction in the letter combinations *ur*, *ea*, and *er*, sound the letters in *nurse*, *someone*, *nose*, *ear*, *peanut*, and *water*, and without help identify each word correctly. Their ears told them what adaptation was required to form words they knew. You needn't therefore feel that your pupil will be lost without special guidance for every word containing a deviation from what has already been taught. Your child's ear is our ally. He or she will soon learn to bend, alter, and adapt the letter sounds in new words sufficiently to permit a recognition of each. Here are the first 15 sentences:

1. **PAT the CAT**

2. **SING A SONG**

3. **SIT ON the RED RUG**

4. **CUT the BUN**

5. **the DOG HAD A NAP**

6. **the TAP DRIPS**

7. **DON'T STEP ON the ANTS**

8.   **STOP the PUP**

9.   **PICK UP the TACK**

10. **thAT BUS IS BIG**

11. **the SUN IS HOT**

12. **thIS STRING IS STRONG**

13. **the PIG IS ON the BED**

14. **the POT HAS A TOP**

15. **the CUB IS IN the TUB**

Learning to read sentences is difficult work for a beginner. Don't expect speedy progress. Be patient and praise your pupil lavishly for every small triumph. We want reading to be a pleasure: a goal that could be jeopardized if we attempt to hurry a child along too quickly or burden him or her with new material too soon. When — and *only* when — your pupil is brimming with confidence from reading the first fifteen sentences, begin the next section.

The blocks game will serve admirably to advance your child's skill in reading sentences. When your youngster is able to read sentences 1 and 2, print these sentences on separate slips, attach them to blocks, and have the child play a game. As your child learns to read each subsequent new sentence, add it to the game on another block or by doubling up sentences on blocks. In time, replace those slips containing sentences that have been well learned.

Throughout this chapter, the learning progression is broken down into a series of steps. Resist the urge to move ahead too quickly with new material. Keep in mind the caution expressed on page 47 concerning the two forms of advancement. Nothing is ever lost —

and much is often gained — by constantly reviewing material already covered.

Step 2: Lower-case letters

It's time now to switch to lower-case or "small" letters. Place a piece of paper over the column of sentences on page 163. Have your learner attempt to read the sentences on page 162. Help when necessary. But always provide *minimal* help — this is important. Don't immediately read a difficult word for your child: he or she will learn nothing by your effort. Instead, give voice to the sound of each new squiggle-shape. If your child continues to falter, uncover the sentence on page 163 for him or her to read. In this way, your child can still take pride in his or her reading ability and gain practice, even though the main object of the exercise isn't completely fulfilled.

An acceptable form of "help" is to read aloud with your pupil, but with your voice always trailing fractionally behind. You aren't really helping at all, but the child will take comfort in believing he or she isn't tackling the job alone.

If your pupil manages to read a sentence on page 162 — perhaps even without your help — don't immediately drop down to the next sentence below. Instead, have your youngster repeat the sentence a couple of times. If this is done with humor, your child won't mind how many times he or she repeats the material. One way to ensure cooperation in repeating a sentence is to say something along the line of, "M-m-m, well, you certainly did a great job that time, Augustine, but I don't think you could get it right twice in a row." Of course, your challenge will be quickly seized upon. Then, into theatrics. Express amazement. "Well, I didn't think . . . but you've probably forgotten it now." Picking up the scent of an easy triumph, the child will launch gleefully into a third reading of the sentence. "If you get it right once more, I'm just going to have to tell Daddy (or Aunt Mary or ???) about this." The vocabulary used in the above examples will have to be simplified, of course, for two- and three-year-olds. But they will rise to the same bait.

Pat the cat . . . .

Sing a song . . . .

Sit on the red rug. . . . .

Cut the bun . . . .

The dog had a nap . . . .

The tap drips . . . .

Don't step on the ants. . . . .

Stop the pup . . . .

Pick up the tack. . . . .

That bus is big . . . .

The sun is hot . . . .

This string is strong . . . .

The pig is on the bed . . . . . .

The pot has a top. . . . .

The cub is in the tub. . . . . . .

When your pupil can easily read all the sentences on this page, move ahead to step 3.

Step 3: Silly sentence review
When children have read the same sentence a few times they may

. . . . PAT the CAT

. . . . SING A SONG

. . . . SIT ON the RED RUG

. . . . CUT the BUN

. . . . the DOG HAD A NAP

. . . . the TAP DRIPS

. . . . DON'T STEP ON the ANTS

. . . . STOP the PUP

. . . . PICK UP the TACK

. . . . thAT BUS IS BIG

. . . . the SUN IS HOT

. . . . thIS STRING IS STRONG

. . . . the PIG IS ON the BED

. . . . the POT HAS A TOP

. . . . the CUB IS IN the TUB

develop the habit of reading only the first word or two, and then *reciting* the rest of the sentence. To counter this habit, I have provided for each new group of sentences a second group, with the same words forming different sentences. These additional sentences are often absurd; however, humor is never lost on children. One caution: never advance to the silly sentence reviews until your pupil can read the preceding material skilfully, else much of the value of the reviews will be lost. Here are the next fourteen sentences.

16. **Pat the red rug.**

17. **The tap had a nap.**

18. **The sun is on a string.**

19. **This pig has a hot dog.**

20. **That bus is in the tub.**

21. **That pup is strong.**

22. **Stop the bed.**

23. **The ant has a big pick.**

24. **That cat has a pot.**

25. **The cub drips.**

26. **Cut up that song.**

27. **Don't sit on that tack.**

28. **Don't step on the top.**

29. **Don't sing on the bun.**

You can always lengthen your silly sentence review — and increase both humor and interest — by making up more sentences using the words that have now been learned. Your pupil will probably become an enthusiastic collaborator in mixing and matching words to form absurd sentences for you to print or type on a separate sheet. Here are some examples:

Don't sit on that bun.

The pig is on the bus.

The sun had a nap.

Pat the hot dog.

The possibilities are numerous — the sillier, the better. Best of all, the longer you dwell on each set of newly learned words, the more quickly will your pupil's reading skill advance. One more caution: for the moment, don't include any new words in the sentences you create.

When your pupil can read sentences 16 to 29 without hesitation, proceed with the next material.

Enlarging your child's vocabulary

If your pupil is only two or three years old, he or she may not know some of the words that will begin to appear in the sentences: words such as *valentine, wedding, fig, jazz,* and *vet* (for *veterinarian*). Without knowing the meaning of these words, your pupil couldn't possibly understand the meaning of any sentence in which the words appear (in the same way he or she wouldn't understand any *spoken* sentence in which they are used). Scout ahead and list words your child may not know, then hold a few lessons in vocabulary growth.

If we merely tell a child the meaning of a new word, he or she may soon forget the word. However, we can greatly increase the likelihood of remembering if we employ a few memory-strengthening procedures.

First, we explain the meaning of a word, taking care to use no words in our explanation that the child doesn't already know. "A veterinarian, Trillium, is a doctor who takes care of animals. Can you say *veterinarian?*" Because the word is long, the child may need help in repeating it. After an eventual success, have the child repeat the word a few more times, solely for the jaw gymnastics. "Good, that's wonderful. A veterinarian is a doctor who takes care of animals. And sometimes, instead of saying *veterinarian*, people just say *vet*." Get her to say both *veterinarian* and *vet*. Then associate the word with an animal known to the child. "When Mrs. Garfunkel's dog, Spot, is sick, where would she take him, Trillium?" She responds.

This still isn't enough. Remember the house, the grass, and the clearing in the introduction to part 2? Fifteen minutes later, broach the matter of the veterinarian again. Then, an hour later, raise the matter once more, and finally, at bed-time, chat up Spot's healer again. In this way, the child is far more likely to remember both *veterinarian* and *vet*. (The latter appears in sentences 94 and 101.)

And what do you do the next day? Right! You mention *veterinarian* and *vet* again.

Step 4: F, f, ee, -y

Now we begin to introduce the letters not yet dealt with. Other letter novelties will be included so that the sentences we form won't seem stilted or unnatural. For example, in the next six sentences, the novelties take the form of double *E*'s, *Y*-endings, and the words *are* and *fence*. Help your pupil with each. And remember, the first day your pupil sees a new letter or combination of letters, he or she merely becomes acquainted with it. And information so fresh in mind today may easily be forgotten two weeks from now. So, as you proceed with new material, periodically return and have your pupil re-read the earlier sentences.

The letter **F** is the first new letter. **F** is sounded *without* voice — just the sound of air escaping as you press your lower lip against your upper teeth. Try it, practise it, and then help your child with the words in which **F** appears.

In *referee*, your pupil encounters for the first time the *er* letter combination. Don't get involved with rules of pronunciation. Just say, "Here, we say **ur**."

In *Frank*, the letter **K** conveys the sound of **C**, unaccompanied by **C** for the first time. If your pupil has trouble, just say, "Here we say *Cuh*."

30. **Frog's feet are funny.**

31. **The fat referee is fast.**

32. **Is this toffee free?**

33. **Get off the fence, Frank.**

34. **Figs are soft and sticky.**

35. **Is this stuff pig's-feed?**

Step 5: Silly sentence review

36. **Get off the toffee, Frank.**

37. **Figs are fat and fast.**

38. **This fence is soft and sticky.**

39. **Is this pig's-feed funny?**

40. **Frog's feet are free.**

41. **The referee is stuffed.**

When — and only when — your pupil can read the above sentences quickly, easily, and exuberantly, proceed with the next material. Always let your youngster enjoy a period of triumph and revel in showing you how smart he or she is before you introduce new, more difficult material.

Step 6: L, l

Next we deal with the letter **L**: not *el*, but a steady voiced tone that ends *before* your tongue leaves the roof of your mouth.

Your pupil will probably be confused to see that the lower-case version of **L** is the same as the upper-case version of **i**. There is no logical explanation for this, so simply resort to the phrase, "Here we say . . ." Help your learner (if necessary) with the new sound given to **A** in *ball*, and in decoding *terribly*.

42.   **Let's lift the block.**

43.   **The old hen has lost an egg.**

44.   **Don't lick the golf ball.**

45.   **This doll is terribly ill.**

46.   **Let's see the black clock.**

47.   **The little bunny is asleep.**

Step 7: Silly sentence review

48.   **Don't lick the old hen.**

49.   **This black clock is terribly ill.**

50.   **The little block is asleep.**

51.   **The bunny has lost its doll.**

52.   **Let's lift the golf ball.**

53.   **This black egg is terrible.**

Step 8: M, m

The letter **M** is next, sounded not as *em*, but just a steady humming sound that ends *before your lips part*. The word *my* may require a brief explanation.

54. **My mitts are muddy.**

55. **I must mop the floor.**

56. **This mat is a mess.**

57. **My milk smells funny.**

58. **The man has a sick lamb.**

59. **Hum a merry song.**

Step 9: Silly sentence review

60. **My mitts are humming.**

61. **I must mop the lamb.**

62. **This mat is merry.**

63. **The man smells a sick floor.**

64. **This song is muddy.**

65. **My milk is a funny mess.**

Step 10: J, j
Time now for **J** — sounded not as *jay*, but the sound of *just* if you leave
the *ust* off. Help your pupil with the words *these, radio,* and *jackrabbits.*

66.   **Are these jars of jam?**

67.   **Don't jiggle the jelly.**

68.   **Jump into this jacket.**

69.   **Mending jugs is a big job.**

70.   **Jackrabbits don't jog.**

71.   **This radio is just junk.**

Step 11: Silly sentence review

72.   **Jump into the big jugs.**

73.   **Don't jiggle the radio.**

74.   **Don't jog on the jelly.**

75.   **Are these jars of junk?**

76.   **Mending jam is just a job.**

77.   **Jacket the jackrabbit.**

Step 12: W
Now we introduce **W**: a voiced sound made while pursing the lips to

say *oo*. If you stop to think about it, any word beginning with a **W** begins with an *oo* sound. Try it, making a quick transition from the *oo* sound to that which follows the hyphen: *oo-indow*, *oo-est*, *oo-inter* (*window*, *west*, *winter*). Coach your pupil accordingly.

78. **The wagon wheels are white.**

79. **Winnie the Pooh went walking.**

80. **Where will the donkey sleep?**

81. **The dog wants some water.**

82. **We won't worry if we don't win.**

83. **This waffle smells sweet.**

Step 13: Silly sentence review

84. **Some waffles went walking.**

85. **Winnie the Pooh wants a donkey.**

86. **We won't win if we smell.**

87. **Don't worry if the wagon sleeps.**

88. **This white water is sweet.**

89. **Where is the dog wheeling?**

Step 14: V, I, you

The next letter is **V**, sounded not as *vee*, but the sound made by touching the upper teeth with the lower lip, smiling, and humming a steady tone.

    The following sentences contain two novelties: the words *I* and *you*. One way to help children remember the word *you* is to print *you* in large letters, then draw a happy face in the *O* and say, "That's *you*," (meaning the happy face is the child's face). There is no point in attempting a detailed explanation for the double *O* in *good* because the sound of double *O* can vary (as in *food*). Don't feel obliged to explain the question mark if your child is very young.

90.   **I will give you a valentine.**

91.   **Vanilla is a flavor.**

92.   **Every minivan is very big.**

93.   **Have you a television set?**

94.   **My dog visits the vet.**

95.   **We have trees in the valley.**

Step 15: Silly sentence review

96.   **I will give you my valley.**

97.   **A dog is in every tree.**

98.   **Have we the valentines?**

99.   **This flavor is minivan.**

100. **Is vanilla on television?**

101. **This is a very big vet.**

Step 16: X

The sound of the letter **X** is the same as a combination of the letters **K** and **S**. If that surprises you, substitute *KS* for an **X** in any word and you achieve the same sound value: *ox/oks, sax/saks*, and so on. We therefore sound the letter **X**, not as *eks*, but just *ks* — which may take a bit of practice. It's like saying *kiss* and leaving out the *i*.

102. **Where is Rex, the ox?**

103. **The fox sees the duck.**

104. **Can you fix this ax?**

105. **The sax is in the box.**

106. **This wax is extra soft.**

107. **Don't mix the six cups.**

Step 17: Silly sentence review

108. **Where is Rex — in the box?**

109. **Wax the six ducks.**

110. **The ox fixed the can.**

111. **This cup is extra soft.**

112. **Don't mix the foxes.**

113. **Don't bang the sax with the ax.**

Step 18: Z
The letter **Z** represents not the sounds *zee* or *zed*, but just a buzzing sound — one we associate with bees.

114. **Where is the Wizard of Oz?**

115. **Let's listen to jazz.**

116. **My bear is very fuzzy.**

117. **My zipper got stuck at the plaza.**

118. **They have a zebra at the zoo.**

119. **This pop has plenty of fizz.**

Step 19: Silly sentence review

120. **My bear got stuck in the fizz.**

121. **The Wizard of Oz is at the plaza.**

122. **Listen, my zipper is popping.**

123. **Let's go and see mud at the zoo.**

124. **This is very fuzzy jazz.**

125. **Zebras drink plenty, don't they?**

Step 20: QU
The letter **Q** is rarely used without an accompanying **U**, so we teach
them together. **QU** conveys a sound that is equivalent to the letter
combinations *CW* or *KW* and, because you already know how to sound
C and **W** correctly, you should have little trouble giving the appropriate sound value to **QU**, which is *koo*. Test the truth of this assertion
with *koo-ick*, *koo-een*, *koo-estion* (*quick*, *queen*, *question*). Your learner
may need help with *mice* and *quarterback*.

126. **The queen is very quiet.**

127. **I have a simple question.**

128. **Mice squeak, ducks quack.**

129. **Don't squeeze the squirrel.**

130. **Let's have a quick quiz.**

131. **The quarterback just quit.**

Step 21: Silly sentence review

132. **The queen is very simple.**

133. **Don't squeeze the question.**

134. **The quick duck just quit.**

135. **Don't quack at the quarterback.**

136. **Mice are quizzing the squirrels.**

137. **I have a quiet squeak.**

All the letters have now been introduced, and your pupil is reading at the level of children at the Institute who have completed our *Primer* and *First Reader*. We will now proceed with the material contained in our *Second Reader*, which deals with various combinations of letters.

You might wonder at what school-grade level your child is now reading. This is difficult to judge because reading levels vary from district to district: children whose reading is rated as grade 1 at one school might be rated at a grade 2, 3, or even 4 level at another school. A good reading program can make all the difference. Still, if we regard the grade levels assigned to school materials by their publishers as being accurate, then we can safely say your youngster is now reading at least at the level of a child who has completed grade 2.

Introducing letter combinations
Your child now needs to learn that some letters change their sounds when they are paired with certain other letters. These include combinations such as *S* and *H*: *sh*, *P* and *H*: *ph*, *C* and *H*: *ch*, and all the other mixes we accept as routine in our language. Bear in mind that a few don't fit neatly into categories; who among us wasn't stumped when we first encountered *canoe*, *viscount*, *yacht*, and other puzzlers? But generally, the orthography of the English language (the way our language is expressed by written or printed symbols) handles most cases well, despite attempts to prove our language isn't phonically based. Advocates of this notion point to the several sounds the letters *ough* can represent — as in *bough*, *cough*, *rough*, *through*, *though*, and possibly a few other words that don't come readily to mind. But the unswerving regularity with which critics seize upon the *ough* combination to prove their point stands as proof that its irregularity is unique; no other letter combinations provide a convincing argument to support their contention.

Your child has already encountered a few letter combinations. We couldn't avoid this and still make the sentence examples interesting. The *ER* combination appeared in *referee* and *zipper*; the *AR* in *are, jars,* and *wizard*; the *OO* in *Pooh*; the *SION* in *television*; the *OR* in *flavor,* and *TION* in *question.* But now it's time to look at letter combinations more thoroughly.

When you are explaining letter combinations, if your child knows the names of the letters (*ay, bee, see,* etc.) you can refer to letters in the combinations by those names. Or, you could as easily refer to the letters by the sound values your child has been taught. We begin with the combination of **O** and **W**; so, you might say *awe* and *oo* make *ow*. Print the letter combination and exercise your child in making the correct sound while running a finger beneath the letters, then help him read the following sentences.

Step 22: OW

138. **The clown has a towel.**

139. **Do owls howl or meow?**

140. **How now, brown cow?**

If the name of a relative, neighbor, or friend contains the **OW** letter combination (as may the street you live on, or the city or town you live in), add these words to your exercise as a small extra study-list — but *not* if the **OW** combination conveys the sound in *blow*, a sound we will deal with later. The more **OW** words you are able to add to your list, the more likely your pupil will quickly learn and remember the **OW** combination. And if you can personalize your silly sentences, all the better. For example, if your pupil has an Uncle Howie, you might type or print the silly sentence, *Does Uncle Howie howl or meow?*

When your child is able to deal comfortably with the **OW** letter combination, proceed with the next combination — **SH**.

Step 23: SH

141. **I wish we had some shells.**

142. **Shall we rush to the shop?**

143. **She has a dish of fresh fish.**

Step 24: IR

144. **Birds don't wear shirts.**

145. **The girl has a skirt.**

146. **Don't get dirty on your birthday.**

Step 25: AI

147. **I'm not afraid of rain on my hair.**

148. **Wait for me on the stairs, Claire.**

149. **The tooth fairy travels by train.**

Step 26: OU

150. **A mouse is running around the house.**

151. **A scout is shouting outside.**

152. **Clouds aren't often found on the ground.**

Step 27: OR

153. **Gorillas are born in the forest.**

154. **This horse eats popcorn with a fork.**

155. **Sorry, but the horn on our Ford snores.**

Step 28: OI

156. **There is oil in the soil.**

157. **Don't drop coins in the toilet.**

158. **Smoking can spoil your voice.**

Step 29: AY

159. **Step this way to the crayon tray.**

160. **It's a gray May day today.**

161. **Is it okay to play outside?**

Step 30: EA

162. **Don't eat the cream, please.**

163. **Don't scream at the meat, heat it.**

164. **I think reading is really easy.**

Step 31: OA

165. **A goat is eating soap in the boat.**

166. **There's a toad on the road.**

167. **Have some roast beef on toast.**

Step 32: CH

168. **The teacher has cherries and chocolate.**

169. **Have a chicken or cheese sandwich.**

170. **You have some lunch on your chin and cheek.**

Step 33: UR

171. **Don't eat cheeseburgers in church, Burt.**

172. **If the burn hurts, see the nurse.**

173. **She lost a purple purse on Thursday.**

Step 34: OW

Now we will deal with the second sound the **OW** combination can convey. Explain to your pupil that the **O** and **W** combination are sometimes sounded differently from the way already learned.

174. **Throw bread on the snow for the sparrows.**

175. **Get your elbow out of the bowl.**

176. **Crows grow slowly.**

Step 35: PH

177. **An elephant is on the telephone.**

178. **This is a photo of a pheasant.**

179. **Phillip, Rudolph, and Daphne are friends.**

Step 36: EW

180. **I have a few cashew nuts.**

181. **Don't chew the screw, Andrew.**

182. **The ship has a new crew.**

Step 37: ER

183. **Gert's perfume is superb.**

184. **A mermaid is a sea person.**

185. **Elephant herds are certainly noisy.**

Step 38: AW

186. **There's a hawk on the lawn.**

187. **Today, I saw the dawn.**

188. **Draw a strawberry.**

Step 39: UE

189. There is glue on this tissue.

190. Ducks can swim: true or untrue?

191. Rescue the blue hippopotamus.

Step 40: GH

192. Don't laugh as you cough.

193. Is there enough pig-feed in the trough?

194. Football is a rough and tough game.

Step 41: KN

195. Cut the knot with the knife.

196. Did you know I can knit?

197. When I kneel my knee hurts.

Step 42: OY

198. The small boy has a large toy.

199. **Don't annoy Her Royal Highness.**

200. **Do cowboys eat soybeans?**

Step 43: WR

201. **What's wrong with your wrist?**

202. **There is writing on the wrapper.**

204. **Don't wreck the wrench.**

CONGRATULATIONS!

There are still a few letter combinations we haven't dealt with, among them **GN** (as in *gnat* and *gnaw*) and **PS** (as in *psychic* and *psychology*), but such combinations usually occur in words that are beyond a young child's immediate vocabulary needs. When these and other less common letter combinations are eventually encountered, you can easily explain them.

I say *easily* because you are now an accomplished teacher. Does that surprise you? Accept it as fact. You have demonstrated uncommon skill in teaching reading. Yes, you had a book to help you, but all professional educators have books to help them. So you needn't feel you are an imposter when I welcome you to the inner circle of reading experts. If you wish to broaden your understanding of the science of reading, you might read the chapter for schoolteachers (chapter 6).

Finally, a word about the rules of pronunciation. I have never attached much importance to these rules, though many educators do. I feel that rules are, by their nature, abstractions. Though reading is itself an abstract process, the fewer abstractions we add to the procedure, the better. Children who make good use of their reading ability soon learn what sounds to give to letters in specific instances —

so, they don't need rules. And children who seldom read are likely to forget any rules you teach them for want of practice in using them. I have found the simplest, easiest, and most effective way to give children a mastery of what we term *rules* is to guide them in ways that activate their natural problem-solving abilities. When your child is stumped in sounding the letters of a new word, an appropriate response is, "Here, we say . . ." rather than launch into a lesson on a rule of pronunciation. The child who is motivated to read, and does so, will soon sort out the methods that are commonly used to make printed words express spoken speech.

9

Some Final
Thoughts

The purpose of this book is to show how to teach reading effectively, not to provoke an invidious comparison with the performance of public schools. Still, parents using the simplified phonic system, seeing how quickly children can be taught to read, might wonder why the task is so difficult and the goal so elusive in the hands of professionals. And schoolteachers who have now employed the program in their classrooms, on seeing speedy advancement so easily achieved, may wonder why they had to turn to a non-establishment publication to learn simple, no-fail teaching methods.

Ineffectual educational leadership was dealt with briefly in chapter 6, but the point bears repeating. Indeed, it begs emphasis.

We hear the phrase, "Our future lies with our children" — a simplistic thought, for, if children aren't adequately educated, our future (meaning, really, theirs and that of our country) may be less impressive than anyone would wish. The sobering truth is this: the abundance or dearth of future fortunes will be greatly influenced — indeed, *is being* greatly influenced — by those who set public-school standards of education today. And those in a position to decide these issues have continuously shown a preference for standards that are low and easily achieved. As a consequence, in the name of education many children are merely picking up learning disabilities and handicaps — and worse, a disinclination to pursue learning — a process sometimes called dumbing down. One sees high school students proudly bearing the trappings of learning (diplomas, gowns, flowers) and flushed with the sense of achievement accorded them by school administrators, sometimes to the accompaniment of speeches and applause — serenely unaware that they have received nothing approaching an education. Their honors are ephemeral. Tomorrow, it's back to being an ignoramus, perhaps just another entrant to the ranks of functional illiterates and fringe unemployables.

To say we have good public-school education is, on one foot, naive, and on the other foot, a hoax, depending on which side of the administrative fence the foot is planted. The damage done to children is insidious, seemingly slight today, but pervasive and cumulative: a thriving malady that works to limit the number of vocational options available to youngsters when they reach adulthood. Parents don't always perceive the limitations being placed on their children. Schoolteachers sometimes don't either. And higher up the administrative ladder — does anyone really care? From my personal encounters with administrative movers and shakers, I conclude that they do not.

We have been conditioned to accept a system of administrative ascendancy in education that permits short-sighted, unenterprising — even obstructive and uneducated — people to secure positions of power. Similar faulty leadership in a commercial organization would prompt stockholders to replace the ineffectuals. But the "stockholders" in public education — the taxpayers — have little voice, and any criticism of educational standards raised by parents or politicians is promptly quashed by the reply, "If you want better education, give us more money."

That stops everyone, because no one knows the precise relationship between funding and educational excellence. No one, that is, except a group sitting in the bleachers, marveling at the travesty being played out, a group that, functioning with much less money than public schools are blessed with, nevertheless achieves far higher levels of academic excellence. I speak of those who operate private schools.

What minimal performance have we a right to expect of public schools? Children should learn to read skilfully and use our language correctly in written and spoken form. They should be able to spell correctly and be able to add, subtract, multiply, and divide. Let only this much be achieved, and my personal wish list would be complete. Not much to ask for in the 1,800 or more days children will spend in school before they may legally drop out.

On now to *A Busy Day for Helpful Andrew.*

PART FOUR

YOUR CHILD'S FIRST BOOK

A Busy Day For Helpful Andrew

Now, at last, the most exciting challenge of all: reading a whole book! When your child completes the "Helpful Andrew" stories, perhaps you (the teacher) and I (the teacher's assistant) should shake hands — if only figuratively — on our successful collaboration in a teaching adventure that has given your child entrance to the wondrous world of print.

Story One

Helpful Andrew Cleans the House

Andrew is four years old. He wants to be helpful. His mother, Mrs. Lee, works very hard. Today, Mrs. Lee is working in the garden. She is digging up bricks that Andrew planted. They didn't grow.

Andrew will surprise his mother today.

Andrew will tidy the house. Out comes the vacuum cleaner. Andrew plugs it in. He flicks the switch — Z-Z-Z-Z. Andrew pushes the vacuum cleaner around. Everything is going to be tidy.

Andrew starts with the kitchen counter.

Z-Z-Z-ZIPP — a fork goes into the vacuum cleaner. Z-Z-Z-ZIPP — there goes a spoon. Z-Z-Z-ZIPP — an egg timer. Z-Z-Z-ZIPP — a shopping list. Z-Z-Z-ZIPP-ZIPP-ZIPP — three tea bags. Now the kitchen counter is tidy.

Next, the living room. Z-Z-Z-ZIPP — a ball of wool. Z-Z-Z-ZIPP-ZIPP — two socks. Z-Z-Z-ZIPP — a pencil. Now the living room is tidy.

Andrew takes the vacuum cleaner into the hall. Z-Z-Z-ZUFF-UGGEL — a golf ball won't go in. Z-Z-Z-ZUFF-ZUFF — neither will a picture on the wall. Z-Z-Z-ZUFF-ZUFF — neither will a slipper. Z-Z-Z-ZIPP-ZUFF-ZUFF-ZIPP — there goes the curtain.

Next, the hall table. Z-Z-Z-ZIPP — a glove. Z-Z-Z-ZIPP — another glove. Z-Z-Z-ZIPP — a bottle of perfume. Z-Z-Z-ZIPP-ZIPP-ZIPP-ZIPP — coins and other things. Andrew sneezes — ZUFFLE-UMP — in goes his foot, then his knee, his whole leg, but Z-Z-Z-ZUFF-ZUFF-ZUFF-GRUMBLE-GRUMBLE. The cleaner is stuck. Andrew turns the machine off. He pulls out his leg. Job finished. Time to rest. He turns on the TV set.

Story Two

Helpful Andrew Wallpapers the Hall

Andrew's mother plans to wallpaper the hall. Why? Because Andrew covered it with spray paint. When will she do it? Not today. She is too busy in the yard. She is trying to find her wedding ring and earrings. They are in the vacuum cleaner bag.

Andrew will surprise his mother. He will wallpaper the hall.

Flour and water make a paste. Andrew knows this. That's how he will stick paper to the wall. He stands on a kitchen chair to reach the flour. It drops. Flour all over the floor. Tidy up later. Must get paper on the wall for the surprise.

Andrew goes to the basement. He finds a can of spray glue. Can't find wallpaper. He'll use newspaper.

S-S-S-S — Andrew sprays the glue on the wall. He slaps the paper onto the wall. Forgot about the picture on the wall. It's under the paper. Andrew gets scissors from the kitchen. Nice how his footsteps show in white. He practices making white footprints for a minute. They look nice. Even nicer on the living-room carpet.

Andrew cuts a hole in the newspaper. Now you can see the picture. Good.

The job is finished. Time to rest. He turns on the TV set.

Story Three

Helpful Andrew Does the Laundry

Andrew's mother is tired. She took off his wallpaper with a steam iron. Mrs. Lee needs a rest. She asks Andrew to play quietly while she lies down.

Andrew doesn't want to play. He wants to be helpful. He will surprise his mother.

Andrew will wash the clothes. But there are no dirty clothes. He will wash the shoes instead.

Andrew gets his father's shoes and slippers. Then he gets his mother's shoes and slippers. Then he gets his own running shoes and slippers. Down to the basement. Andrew stands on a chair. He dumps everything into the washing machine.

How much soap should he put in the machine? He doesn't know. There are two boxes of soap. He wants the shoes to be very clean. He empties both boxes of soap into the machine. Everything is ready. Andrew turns the knob. The washing machine starts. Whir-whir-whir-whir.

What will he do now? Andrew thinks. Time to rest. He will sit on the front step until the shoes are washed.

Soon, Andrew's father comes home. His father sees something white and fluffy coming out the windows. Can

you guess what it is?

Story Four

Helpful Andrew Paints the Car

Andrew's father and mother are very busy. They are getting soap suds out of the house. They won't let Andrew help. He will have to help in some other way.

There is rust on the car. He will help by getting rid of the rust. There are spray cans of paint in the garage. What colors are in the cans? Any color would look better than rust. That's what Andrew thinks.

Andrew shakes a can. He pushes the button on the top. Nothing happens. He finds a hammer. Andrew hits the button with the hammer. S-S-S-S. It works. The spray is pointed at him. Now part of Andrew's shirt is a different color. It's red. But he likes red. So he doesn't mind.

Andrew starts painting the rust spots. S-S-S-S. Red looks nice on a white car. Now the spray is stuck again. Andrew hits the button with the hammer. S-S-S-S. Now part of his pants is a different color. But he likes red.

Soon, the paint is all gone. There are still some rust spots. He takes another can of paint. S-S-S-S. It works fine. Blue. He likes blue. Now the car will be red, white, and blue. Job finished.

There is some blue paint left. What can he paint? The grass. Andrew has heard there is blue grass in Kentucky. That's where finger-licking-good fried chickens grow. S-S-S-S. Blue grass looks nice. His blue shoes look nice too.

Story Five

Helpful Andrew Cuts His Hair

Andrew must stay in his room. His mother and father are cleaning the colors off the car. Perhaps Andrew picked the wrong colors. Nobody is perfect.

Andrew is allowed to go as far as the bathroom. He goes. Andrew looks in the mirror. His hair is getting long. Andrew's father cuts Andrew's hair. But his father is always very busy.

Andrew will surprise his father. He will cut his own hair.

The hair clipper is in the drawer. Out it comes. Andrew plugs the clipper in. BUZ-Z-Z-Z. It works. All ready. BUZ-Z-Z-Z-SWISH-ZIPP. One side of his head is finished. This is easy. BUZZ-Z-Z-Z-SWISH-ZIPP. That takes care of the other side. Andrew can't reach the back of his head. Leave it. Too difficult.

What else can he trim? Toothbrush. BUZ-Z-Z-Z. Looks neater now. BUZ-Z-Z-Z. Another neat toothbrush. BUZ-Z-Z-Z. Another. Now the hairbrush. BUZ-Z-Z-Z. Looks cleaner now. Job finished. Someone coming up the stairs. Back to his room quickly.

YOUR CHILD'S READING PROGRAM

Having read the absurdities of the "Helpful Andrew" stories, your child now sees that printed material can be as entertaining as TV, and that it also offers the advantage of instant replay, simply by flicking the eyes up a line or two. In any case, the Helpful Andrew stories merely *introduce* the wonders of print to your child. More is needed if he or she is to advance from the role of a beginning reader to that of an expert reader. Our task now is to engage your child in reading to the point where reading becomes second nature — a habit.

To this end, establish a program that will encourage — nay, lure — your child into the pages of books. Make sure your youngster has within easy reach plenty of interesting, easy-to-read material — interesting, that is, for your child, not for *you*. Some parents would like their child to pore over an encyclopedia, but most children would rather pore over a comic book. Never oblige your child to read text he or she finds boring or difficult. Such an obligation would not promote a love of reading.

And incidentally, don't denigrate or devalue the role that comic books can play in promoting the habit of reading. They serve our immediate goal admirably — which isn't to elevate your child's literary taste (Shakespeare can come later), but merely to get him or her exercising — and exercising *frequently* — the newly acquired ability to process printed material. When your child eventually becomes a highly skilled reader, you can then begin wheeling and dealing for quality reading. In the meantime, visit a store that specializes in comic books. You may be surprised at the wide assortment of material available in this simple picture format — the nearest thing to TV on paper. Take your child along and let him or her choose the books.

Children's books, whether bought or borrowed, should be selected with care. Some flaws to be found in children's books are (1) too little space between lines; (2) columns too wide (narrow columns are easier to read); and (3) use of obscure words (the following words were found in elementary children's books: *twinning, bade, provender, inquiringly, encircling, thrillingly, parasol*). If books are made the means of increasing children's vocabulary, then reading becomes a chore instead of the joy it should be. Later, children may indeed enlarge their vocabularies by reading, but vocabulary building via books shouldn't be an early goal.

Authors of children's books sometimes forget that adult expressions can be puzzling for children; we find *spend the night* used instead of *stay the night* or just plain *sleep there*; *knew better than to* instead of *knew he shouldn't*, and *he went on* for *he said*. Avoidance of adult idioms is especially important while children are reading their first two hundred books.

A witch in one book was described as having "a face like a bad dream," and we shouldn't be surprised if the memory of that creature upset children's sleep. Some fairy tales are peopled by grotesque characters who, if they could be projected onto an adult scale of intimidation, would make most of us sleep with a stout club handy and never climb into bed without first looking under it.

Taste in children's literature probably reaches its lowest point in the perennial favorite, *Hansel and Gretel*, wherein the stepmother and the children's natural father twice condemn the children to slow death by starvation, and then a witch tries to roast them for supper. An adult movie with a plot centered on infanticide by starvation, followed by attempted cannibalism, might get rough reviews.

Children have enough cares just coping with daily uncertainties and complexities without facing a clan of abominable creatures presented in the name of "pleasure" reading. The "big bad wolf" may not bother you and me, but how does he appear through the imaginative eyes of someone who hasn't yet sorted out fact from fiction? I have to admit this confusion didn't occur to me until my own children had met big bad wolves in *Three Little Pigs* and *Little Red Riding Hood*. When I noticed the children developing a morbid fascination for the creatures, I had to point out repeatedly that wolves of this sort lived only in books, and that real wolves try to stay away from people.

Visit the public library regularly with your child. Let him or her experience the awe and fascination that walls and walls of books can generate (and equally important, feel the contentment that special setting can convey). Ask the librarian to help you find books that fascinate children of your child's age. Librarians are keen to promote literacy, and they can direct you to exciting books you might not discover on your own. While at the library, borrow a selection of children's magazines, then subscribe to any that interest your child.

Make reading a bedtime feature for your child, a means of keeping the light on a bit longer. (Of course, the TV and radio should both be switched off.) If you still read to your child at bedtime (an excellent practice even with older children) you might read just enough of a story to arouse your child's curiosity, then hand him or her the book to continue reading to you, or to read alone until it's "lights out."

Obviously, a great amount of TV viewing will greatly reduce the amount of time your child has available for reading. Some parents choose to limit TV time, or make TV viewing conditional upon reading. One parent reported that her child became so absorbed in the reading he didn't trouble to switch on the TV set at the appointed time.

If your child shows a reluctance to read — which is completely normal before reading proficiency is achieved — you would be wise to employ inducements to promote reading. The purchase of something your child longs for — a special toy, equipment, or a visit to a major event or attraction — can be made a prize for a specified amount of reading. Even the purchase of colorful, high-quality bound books the child desires (horses, dogs, aircraft, and cooking are popular) might be included in your reading inducement plan. Make a rough chart, display it on the wall, and with a marker plot your child's steady progress toward securing the desired object. Add razzle-dazzle to your display by affixing a toy car to the chart. The child can then observe the car's daily progress across the chart to the finish line, at which point the desired item becomes his or hers. (You will find that items earned in this way will be treasured more than those that are simply given to a child.)

Though the payment of extraneous rewards for reading isn't always popular with educators, we are using the practice only as a temporary measure to quickly advance your child's reading expertise. The content of the books themselves will eventually provide the intrinsic reward that all who love books share.

Appendix I

The Myth of Dyslexia

My claim, made earlier, that dyslexia is in almost all cases an ailment produced by faulty reading programs may generate resentment, perhaps even outrage, among some educators. (On the other hand, others may sigh with relief on finally seeing their own convictions in print.) In any case, I feel obliged to add substance to my contention that when children fail to learn to read easily and quickly it is usually the method that is at fault, not the pupils, and that it is the reading program that needs remedial treatment, not the children.

But first, what does the word *dyslexia* mean? To some it means merely an inability to read; to others it means an inability *to learn to read* — quite a different matter, implying that no amount of instruction will result in reading ability. And to others the word means having extreme difficulty in learning to read — though perhaps not ruling out the possibility that such children can learn to read if appropriate instruction is provided. This third interpretation harbors a puzzlement we will return to.

Stated simply, the first group of so-called dyslexics are merely unable to read. This would include most children under the age of six.

They can't read because no one has taught them how to. The second group apparently have little more chance of learning to read than do blocks of granite. And the third group? Seemingly there is hope, though fulfilment of that hope is contingent upon the provision of suitable instruction.

Finally, if we add the dictionary definition of dyslexia — "a disturbance of the ability to read," which is both general and ambiguous — we end up riding a semantic merry-go-round on which almost nothing can be proved or disproved. But let's try.

Adhering to the dictionary definition that dyslexia is a disturbance of the ability to read, we must certainly acknowledge its existence, for many schools are well stocked with children who demonstrate a disturbance in learning to read. But this disturbance should never have occurred, and it would *not* have occurred if an effective method of instruction had been employed when the children were first introduced to the mechanics of reading.

Based on my own experience these past thirty years, and on the reports of teacher members of the Reading Reform Foundation — whose goal is to return phonic reading systems to all classrooms — I am convinced that dyslexia is, with few exceptions, the product of faulty reading programs. It is, in short, a manufactured ailment, one initiated by faulty instruction and perpetuated by an incorrect interpretation of the consequences of that faulty instruction — an irrational conclusion based on a misinterpreted failure. And when an erroneous interpretation is made of the failure, and a false conclusion drawn from its manifestation, we leave logic behind and join Alice in a wonderland of fantasy and myth.

Regrettably, the myth of dyslexia has now assumed the mantle of legitimacy, even dignity. *Dyslexia* is, after the overworked terms *learning disability* and *attention deficit disorder*, the next most popular excuse for explaining why children fail to read.

Some reading programs have built-in inoculative powers that prevent the scourge of dyslexia. These programs teach children the sounds of the letters, then engage the youngsters in left-to-right sounding out of the letters, and finally, give children plenty of exercise in both important steps.

These procedures always work — at my Institute and in every classroom they are employed. They work no less well today than they did eighty years ago when the phonic reading method ruled supreme in Canadian public schools. At that time, non-reading schoolchildren were virtually unknown. (However, U.S. schools were already being burdened with the dyslexia-generating look-say or whole word programs favored by the revered educational titan of that period, John Dewey, a name that looms large in the "progressive education" movement.)

The gravamen of misinterpreting the cause of dyslexia is that as soon as a disturbance in reading occurs — "Click!"; with all the expedition of a pool ball dispatched to the side pocket the child is chalked up as the cause. That there might be anything wrong with the instruction is unthinkable.

One reason teaching methods are seldom held suspect is that many children are bright enough, or have sufficient aptitude for learning to read, that they succeed despite the failings of the system. Still others, aided by their parents (who perhaps secure guidance from popular how-to books), learn to read at home. They too are counted among the school's successes. When teachers see so many of their children learning to read, they naturally assume there is nothing wrong with the reading program they are given to use. So, there must be something wrong with those children who fall behind in reading.

The notion that a specified number or percentage of children suffer inhibition in reading is further befuddled by failure to recognize a basic fact: children learn to read (and indeed, learn most matters) with varying ease.

For example, some preschoolers learn to read so easily their parents report that the youngsters taught themselves (a matter dealt with on page 31). On a scale of one to ten, such children would rate a ten for their exceptional aptitude for learning to read. Children with less aptitude would be assigned the numbers nine, eight, seven, and so on, down to one. If a reading program is designed so that only children with aptitudes of two and higher will read, then those with an aptitude of only one (however bright they might be in other ways) are bound to exhibit "a disturbance in the ability to read," in other words, dyslexia.

Excuses for reading failure are just as frequent today as they were in the past, though *fewer* excuses are given (which might loosely be regarded as a form of progress). In her 1947 book, *Why Pupils Fail in Reading*, Professor Helen Robinson, co-author of the fault-filled, whole word Dick-and-Jane readers, assigned no fewer than five pages to list the alleged social, economic, mental, and physical adversities that could hamper reading progress — including (and I'm not kidding) undescended testicles (which might be regarded as a favorable affliction if one were female). Professor Robinson's book might well convince us that "experts" come in all hues, shades, and patterns.

Back to reality. A major failing among many who are adorned with prestigious academic titles is that, though they speculate — indeed, pontificate — on the best way to teach reading, few have ever taught children to read. Let's turn for alternative guidance to one who began as a schoolteacher, and who during a forty-year period visited more than eight hundred classrooms to train student teachers: Patrick Groff, professor of education emeritus at San Diego University, author of the book *Preventing Reading Failures* (Halcyon House, revised edition, 1998) and of more than three hundred articles, reports, and monographs dealing mainly with the conditions that favor or thwart reading ability. Professor Groff states:

> *An overwhelming body of evidence supports the belief that whether children learn to read, and how easily they learn to read, is largely dependent on the method by which they are taught. Reading programs that de-emphasize the connection between letters and the speech-sounds that letters represent nurture faulty reading; then, childen who fail in such programs are labelled dyslexic with the assumption they are not able to learn to read.**

Dr. Ruth Weir, Ph.D. Ed., author of *The Literate Elite* (Lugus Publications, 1997), an exhaustively documented study of the decline of literacy and scholastic standards in the province of Ontario, minces no words about use of the word *dyslexia*.

---

*   Personal correspondence with the author

The term dyslexia is an overworked excuse to hide poor teaching — noth-
ing more. Patience, diligence — a little love helps — and phonic reading
instruction are all it takes to graduate a class of precise and adventurous
grade 1 readers.*

What would anyone with a doctorate in education know about the
front-line challenges and frustrations that junior-grade teachers face
daily in their classrooms? In this case, plenty. Ruth Weir taught grades
1, 2, and 3 for twenty years in three inner-city Toronto schools, with
classes running as high as thirty-five children, the majority of whom
came from non-English-speaking homes.

When Dr. Weir taught grade 1, all her children were reading skilfully by Christmas. I don't mean they were able to recite fifty or sixty
memorized words. No, they had, by then, sufficient mastery of the
letter-sound code to puzzle out the contents of thousands of words.
And when Ruth Weir taught grade 2 or 3, her children (many diehard
guessers from faulty previous instruction) were straightened around
and were similarly reading accurately by Christmas. Not surprisingly,
her classroom became the "fix-it" center for each school in which she
taught. "Let Weir have them," was the operating dictum for children
who were labelled as dyslexic, learning disadvantaged, or suffering
from attention deficit disorder. All the children received the Weir
"magic". All read.

Well, not quite. Of all the children Ruth Weir instructed throughout her teaching career — about six hundred altogether — there were
two she couldn't teach to read. Brian, an unusual child, could leap
out of a second storey window and feel no pain. The products of a
vicious home life, Brian and his brother eventually entered a mental
institution. The other reading failure was José, victim of an automobile
accident, who had suffered brain damage so severe he couldn't
remember matters from one day to the next.

Two failures out of six hundred children! That's 0.3 percent. But wait,
could we say these two children were dyslexic? Possibly. A more

---

*   Personal correspondence with the author

accurate term might be *dysfunctional.* To term children this badly disoriented as being merely dyslexic is an understatement on the order of describing a corpse as being someone in very poor health.

Let's turn to an expert who doesn't agree with me, one who must remain unnamed. During his long career, this man — a professor of psychology emeritus at a major North American university — dealt with 40,000 children who suffered reading difficulties. He stoutly defends use of the term *dyslexia* to describe what he considers to be a naturally occurring deficiency, one suffered by no fewer than five percent of all children. He dismisses my contention that disturbance in the ability to read results from the use of faulty reading programs.

Now the twist. This same expert concedes that even the afflicted five percent can be taught to read if a wholly phonic method is used and if the children receive appropriate individualized instruction.

So where does that leave me? Elated. Without meaning to, the professor has proved my point.

He has confirmed my contention that when a simple phonic program of reading instruction is used, all children — including his "dyslexic" five percent — learn to read. But if his ostensibly deficient dyslexic children learned to read when they were taught sensibly, they weren't deficient in the first place, were they? It was the reading instruction they had previously received that was deficient. Clearly, his unfortunate five percent were the products of dyslexia-promoting reading programs.

CONCLUSION

The fixation with percentages, classification, and terminology confuses the issue and camouflages the basic problems of reading instruction. We end up playing games with numbers and with definitions that few agree on. Wouldn't it be more accurate, and less deceptive, to simply say that some children will have special difficulty learning to read when reading instruction is made unnecessarily complex and when certain vitally important information — instruction in, and practice with, the sounds of the letters — is withheld?

Additionally, in designing any learning system, shouldn't we take into account the fact that children vary greatly in their ability to learn?

Another spook in the system is the fact that children don't learn in the same way adults learn. My book *Teach Your Child to Read in 60 Days* provided ample evidence of the astonishing capacity normal children have for forgetting and becoming puzzled. And of course, it is children themselves, not the experts, who are best suited to decide what teaching procedures will yield the greatest chance of success.

I don't expect all educators to thump the table in thunderous agreement with me. After all, cherished beliefs die hard. But I ask a small favor of all skeptics and dissidents — seek out your own expert. You'll find a few in major cities, and perhaps even one or two in small towns. They are teachers who, like Ruth Weir, use a wholly phonic method of instruction and have their entire grade 1 class reading by Christmas year after year. Ask around. You can find them through the grapevine.

To teach a matter badly, and then fault those who don't learn easily, is reprehensible. Popular use of the term *dyslexia* to explain children's inability to read following faulty instruction is, at best, naive and deceptive, and at worst professionally dishonest.

Let's not be dishonest with children. They have no defence.

APPENDIX II

The Test Used to Identify Early Readers

said	to	down	jump
mother	for	big	house
red	it	in	blue
want	father	here	we
can	is	work	away
help	stop	little	ball
get	and	funny	you
the	come	play	see
look	make	me	go
			not

The ball is red.

Come and look.

Come and see the ball.

It is not big.

It is little and red.

Mother said it is for me.

Index

ISBN 141201554-5